C000180046

LLANDUDNO & COLWYN BAY TRAMWAY

Stephen Lockwood

Series editor Robert J Harley

Front Cover: Palladium Corner in Llandudno was the busiest point on the tram route, particularly in the summer, when hundreds of passengers alighted from and boarded the trams here. Two of the line's second hand trams are seen in this view. On the left is ex Darwen streamline car 23, and on the right ex Bournemouth open top car 15, which has just arrived from Colwyn Bay. For further details see photograph 15. (Roy Brook/Craig Ollerton/Llandudno Enthusiasts)

Rear Cover: This view dates from the very early days of the tramway, and shows a panorama of Rhos on Sea seafront. One of the fleet of single deck cars, in the original maroon and cream livery, turns from Whitehall Road towards the promenade. (Commercial postcard/Geoff Smith coll.)

Cover colours: These reflect the green and cream livery of the tramway.

Published October 2007

ISBN 978 1 906008 17 8

Design Deborah Esher

Published by
Middleton Press
Easebourne Lane
Midhurst
West Sussex
GU29 9AZ
Tel: 01730 813169
Fax: 01730 812601
Email: info@middletonpress.co.uk
www.middletonpress.co.uk

Printed & bound by Biddles Ltd, Kings Lynn

CONTENTS

INTRODUCTION AND ACKNOWLEDGEMENTS

One of the best loved tramways in Great Britain, the Llandudno and Colwyn Bay Electric Railway (L&CBER), began operating on 19th October 1907. When the 6 mile line closed after 49 years service in 1956, it was Britain's last company owned street tramway, its last narrow gauge street tramway and the last street tramway to operate a fleet of traditional open-top double deckers.

The great affection for the L&CBER trams was due to several factors. In its six mile/9.6km length, the line incorporated a vast range of typical British tramway practice. It had single tracks with loops, operation through busy town streets, reserved tracks across rural fields and unmade roads. It ran along country lanes and up a steep hill behind the Little Orme with scenic views over the countryside. Above all, it was a seaside line with very busy seasonal traffic and throughout its length it was always close to the sea – too close at one point as described later. The trams themselves added to the interest, ranging from long interurban style single deckers to open topped double deckers and the holidaymakers' favourites – the open toastracks.

My own interest in the line was kindled three years after the line closed. The Lockwood family's first holiday in Wales was at Rhos on Sea in 1959, when I was ten years old. Arriving at Colwyn Bay station, we decided to walk along the promenade to our boarding house. This was not the arduous trek that it might seem, because our luggage had been sent on some days earlier by that admirable and much missed British Railways service – Passengers' Luggage in Advance. Approaching Rhos I noticed elderly red double deck buses turning off the promenade in the distance. Closer inspection, for these buses passed the door of our boarding house, revealed that they bore no fleetnames, just small lettering painted in neat script by the front wheel which revealed the operator to be the 'Llandudno and Colwyn Bay Electric Railway Limited'. The curious case of a bus service purporting to be an electric railway needed further investigation! By the end of the holiday, I had discovered the redundant tracks at Orme Point, the trackbed at Penrhyn Hill and the depot in Penrhyn Avenue. Ever since that visit, the line has held a great fascination for me and I am extremely grateful to Middleton Press for the chance to present this album.

The detailed history of the tramway has been well documented in previous publications, the first book on the subject, by Roy Anderson, being published in the 1960s. This centenary album is not a definitive history but a pictorial volume with historical information, covering the whole 49 years of operation. The photographs provide a pictorial journey along the entire line.

This project would not have been possible without the help and support of the following, to whom sincere thanks are offered. Geoff Smith, who knew the trams well and is now a Seaton

Tramways driver, and Roy Anderson, who worked on the cars in the late 1940s, have both read through the text and offered advice and suggestions accordingly. Geoff has also made available his extensive collection of commercial postcards of the line. Roger Smith has drawn the excellent detailed map of the system. Terry Russell has prepared and supplied the scale plans of the cars. Eric Old and Stephen Howarth provided the examples of tickets. The photograph on the front cover was made available by Craig Ollerton, founder of the Llandudno Enthusiasts' website, to which lovers of the resort are recommended (www.Olle.co.uk). Richard and Anne Wiseman gave me free choice from their extensive collection of L&CBER material. The many providers of photographs, who all readily responded to my requests, are individually credited in the captions.

Thanks are also due to the staff of the Conwy Archive Service, based in Lloyd Street, Llandudno, for their great efforts to assist me with my researches. The Archive holds the collection of the Llandudno and Colwyn Bay Tramway Society (L&CBTS), for which Geoff Price and Bob Barnsdale deserve credit. Photographs and documents from this collection are reproduced here.

The information regarding L&CBER tram parts incorporated in trams at Seaton is taken from an article by Andrew Simpson published in 'Tramway Review' dated September 2005, and is reproduced here with the kind permission of the editor and author.

Lastly, I have to thank my wife Eileen, who, as ever, tries to ensure that my grammar and spelling are up to standard.

Note: The images credited to Dr HA Whitcombe are now held in the Whitcombe Collection at The Science Museum (www.nmsi.ac.uk).

GEOGRAPHICAL SETTING

The two holiday resorts of Llandudno and Colwyn Bay (Bae Colwyn) are 5 miles apart on the North Wales coast, approximately half way between Chester and Holyhead. Between the two resorts is situated the smaller seaside town of Rhos on Sea. Llandudno lies on a promontory beneath the limestone headland of Great Orme's Head (familiarly known as the 'Great Orme'). A cable tramway from the town to the summit was opened in 1902, and this still operates in summer months. The town has two shorelines – to the east is Llandudno Bay and ¾ mile to the west is West Shore overlooking the Conwy estuary. Further east, towards Colwyn Bay, is a lesser limestone headland called Little Orme's Head (the 'Little Orme'). In tramway days, Llandudno was in Caernarvonshire and Colwyn Bay in Denbighshire, the boundary being crossed by the route of the tramway at Marine Drive, Rhos. Today, the whole area lies within Conwy County Borough Council's jurisdiction.

DA 7919
LLANDUDNO & COLWYN BAY ELECTRIC RLY. LTD.

Stage		Stage
1		6
2		5
3		4
4		3
5		2
6		1

Ticket is to be punched in the section to which Passenger is entitled to travel, and must be shown on demand. Issued subject to the Bye-laws.

AUTO-TICKETS LTD. BIRKENHEAD

I 7414
LLANDUDNO & COLWYN BAY ELECTRIC RLY. LTD.

Stage		Stage
1		6
2		5
3		4
4		3
5		2
6		1

Ticket is to be punched in the section to which Passenger is entitled to travel, and must be shown on demand. Issued subject to the Bye-laws.

AUTO-TICKETS LTD. BIRKENHEAD

G 8003
LLANDUDNO & COLWYN BAY ELECTRIC RLY. LTD.

Stage		Stage
1		6
2		5
3		4
4		3
5		2
6		1

Ticket is to be punched in the section to which Passenger is entitled to travel, and must be shown on demand. Issued subject to the Bye-laws.

AUTO-TICKETS LTD. BIRKENHEAD

UNTIL FURTHER NOTICE.

LLANDUDNO AND COLWYN BAY ELECTRIC RAILWAY LIMITED

TIME  TABLE

LLANDUDNO TO COLWYN BAY — WEEKDAYS

	am	am	am	am	am	am	am	am	am	am	am	am	am		pm	pm		pm	pm	pm	pm
West Shore	...	...	7 15	...	7 45	...	8 15	...	8 45	9 0	9 15	...	9 45	Then every 15 mins. Church Rd. and C. Bay and every 30 mins. Llandudno and C. Bay	...	6 45	Then every 30 mins. until	9 45	10 15	10 45	...
Palladium Corner	...	...	7 18	...	7 51	...	8 21	...	8 51	9 6	9 21	...	9 51		...	6 51		9 51	10 21	10 49	...
Queen's Road	...	...	7 24	...	7 58	...	8 28	...	8 58	9 13	9 28	...	9 58		...	6 58		9 58	10 28	10 56	...
Little Orme Cafe	...	7 20	7 31	...	8 5	...	8 35	...	9 5	9 20	9 35	...	10 5		...	7 5		10 5	10 35	11 3	...
Maesgwyn Road	...	7 23	7 33	...	8 8	...	8 38	...	9 8	9 23	9 38	...	10 8		...	7 8		10 8	10 38	11 6	...
Church Road	7 5	7 26	7 36	7 56	8 11	8 26	8 41	8 56	9 11	9 26	9 41	9 56	10 11		6 56	7 11		10 11	10 41	11 10	...
Cayley Arms	7 9	7 33	7 40	8 3	8 18	8 33	8 48	9 3	9 18	9 33	9 48	10 3	10 18		7 3	7 18		10 18	10 48		...
King's Road	7 14	7 38	7 45	8 8	8 23	8 38	8 53	9 8	9 23	9 38	9 53	10 8	10 23		7 8	7 23		10 23	10 53	...	...
Greenfield Road	7 20	7 43	7 50	8 13	8 28	8 43	8 58	9 13	9 28	9 43	9 58	10 13	10 28		7 13	7 28		10 28	10 58	...	...

COLWYN BAY TO LLANDUDNO — WEEKDAYS

	am	am	am	am	am	am	am	am	am	am	am	am	am		pm	pm		pm	pm	pm	pm
Greenfield Road	...	...	...	7 30	7 45	8 0	8 15	8 30	8 45	9 0	9 15	9 30	9 45	Then every 15 mins. C. Bay and Church Road and every 30 mins. C. Bay and Llandudno	7 15	7 30	Then every 30 minutes until	10 0	10 30	11 0	...
St. Paul's	...	...	...	7 32	7 47	8 2	8 17	8 32	8 47	9 2	9 17	9 32	9 47		7 17	7 32		10 2	10 31	11 1	...
King's Road	...	...	...	7 35	7 49	8 5	8 20	8 35	8 49	9 5	9 19	9 35	9 49		7 19	7 35		10 5	10 34	11 4	...
Cayley Arms	...	...	...	7 40	7 54	8 10	8 25	8 40	8 54	9 10	9 24	9 40	9 54		7 24	7 40		10 10	10 38	11 8	...
Church Road	6 50	7 15	7 20	7 45	7 56	8 15	8 30	8 45	8 56	9 15	9 26	9 45	9 56		7 26	7 45		10 15	10 40	11 10	...
Maesgwyn Road	6 53	7 17	7 23	7 49		8 19	8 34	8 49		9 19		9 49	...			7 49		10 19			...
Little Orme Cafe	6 55	7 19	7 25	7 52	...	8 22	8 37	8 52	...	9 22	...	9 52	...		...	7 52		10 22	...	...	...
Queen's Road	7 2		7 32	8 0	...	8 30	8 45	9 0	...	9 30	...	10 0	...		...	8 0		10 30	...	...	...
Palladium Corner	7 10	...	7 40	8 10	...	8 40	8 55	9 10	...	9 40	...	10 10	...			8 10		10 40	...	...	...
West Shore	7 13	...	7 43	8 13	...	8 43	8 58	9 13	...	9 43	...	10 13				8 13		10 43	...	...	...

The Local Service, Church Road—Colwyn Bay, does not run on Wednesdays after 1.0 p.m. from Church Road and 1.15 p.m. from Greenfield Road.

LLANDUDNO TO COLWYN BAY — SUNDAYS ONLY

	pm	pm	pm	pm	pm	pm	pm	pm	pm	pm	pm	pm	pm	pm	pm	pm	pm	pm	pm	pm	pm
West Shore	...	...	...	...	3 20	3 50	4 20	4 50	5 20	5 50	6 20	6 50	7 20	7 50	8 20	8 50	9 20	9 50	...	...	...
Palladium Corner	...	...	...	...	3 26	3 56	4 26	4 56	5 26	5 56	6 26	6 56	7 26	7 56	8 26	8 56	9 24	9 56	...	...	...
Queen's Road	...	...	...	...	3 33	4 3	4 33	5 3	5 33	6 3	6 33	7 3	7 33	8 3	8 33	9 3	9 31	10 3	...	...	...
Little Orme Cafe	...	...	...	...	3 40	4 10	4 40	5 10	5 40	6 10	6 40	7 10	7 40	8 10	8 40	9 10	9 38	10 10	...	...	...
Maesgwyn Road	...	...	...	...	3 43	4 13	4 43	5 13	5 43	6 13	6 43	7 13	7 43	8 13	8 43	9 13	9 41	10 13	...	...	...
Church Road	...	...	2 50	3 20	3 46	4 16	4 46	5 16	5 46	6 16	6 46	7 16	7 46	8 16	8 46	9 16	9 45	10 16	...	...	...
Cayley Arms	...	...	2 54	3 24	3 53	4 23	4 53	5 23	5 53	6 23	6 53	7 23	7 53	8 23	8 53	9 23	...	10 23	...	...	...
King's Road	...	...	2 58	3 28	3 58	4 28	4 58	5 28	5 58	6 28	6 58	7 28	7 58	8 28	8 58	9 28	...	10 28	...	...	...
Greenfield Road	...	...	3 3	3 33	4 3	4 33	5 3	5 33	6 3	6 33	7 3	7 33	8 3	8 33	9 3	9 33	...	10 33	...	...	...

COLWYN BAY TO LLANDUDNO — SUNDAYS ONLY

	pm	pm	pm	pm	pm	pm	pm	pm	pm	pm	pm	pm	pm	pm	pm	pm	pm	pm	pm	pm	pm
Greenfield Road	...	...	3 5	3 35	4 5	4 35	5 5	5 35	6 5	6 35	7 5	7 35	8 5	8 35	9 5	9 35	10 35	...	...	...	...
St. Paul's	...	...	3 7	3 37	4 7	4 37	5 7	5 37	6 7	6 37	7 7	7 37	8 7	8 37	9 7	9 36	10 36	...	...	...	...
King's Road	...	...	3 10	3 40	4 10	4 40	5 10	5 40	6 10	6 40	7 10	7 40	8 10	8 40	9 10	9 39	10 39	...	...	...	...
Cayley Arms	...	...	3 15	3 45	4 15	4 45	5 15	5 45	6 15	6 45	7 15	7 45	8 15	8 45	9 15	9 43	10 43	...	...	...	...
Church Road	2 55	3 25	3 19	3 50	4 20	4 50	5 20	5 50	6 20	6 50	7 20	7 50	8 20	8 50	9 20	9 45	10 45	...	...	...	...
Maesgwyn Road	2 58	3 28	...	3 54	4 24	4 54	5 24	5 54	6 24	6 54	7 24	7 54	8 24	8 54	9 24	...	...	...	...	...	...
Little Orme Cafe	3 0	3 30	...	3 57	4 27	4 57	5 27	5 57	6 27	6 57	7 27	7 57	8 27	8 57	9 27	...	...	...	...	...	...
Queen's Road	3 7	3 37	...	4 4	4 34	5 4	5 34	6 4	6 34	7 4	7 34	8 4	8 34	9 4	9 34	...	...	...	...	...	...
Palladium Corner	3 14	3 44	...	4 14	4 44	5 14	5 44	6 14	6 44	7 14	7 44	8 14	8 44	9 14	9 44	...	...	...	...	...	...
West Shore	3 18	3 48	...	4 18	4 48	5 18	5 48	6 18	6 48	7 18	7 48	8 18	8 48	9 18	9 48	...	...	...	...	...	...

The Company reserves the right to vary or cancel the above Time Table without previous notice, and shall not be responsible for any delay or inconvenience from any cause whatsoever.

NOVEMBER, 1952.

H. T. JONES, Assistant Manager.

POWLSONS, THE COLWYN BAY PRESS

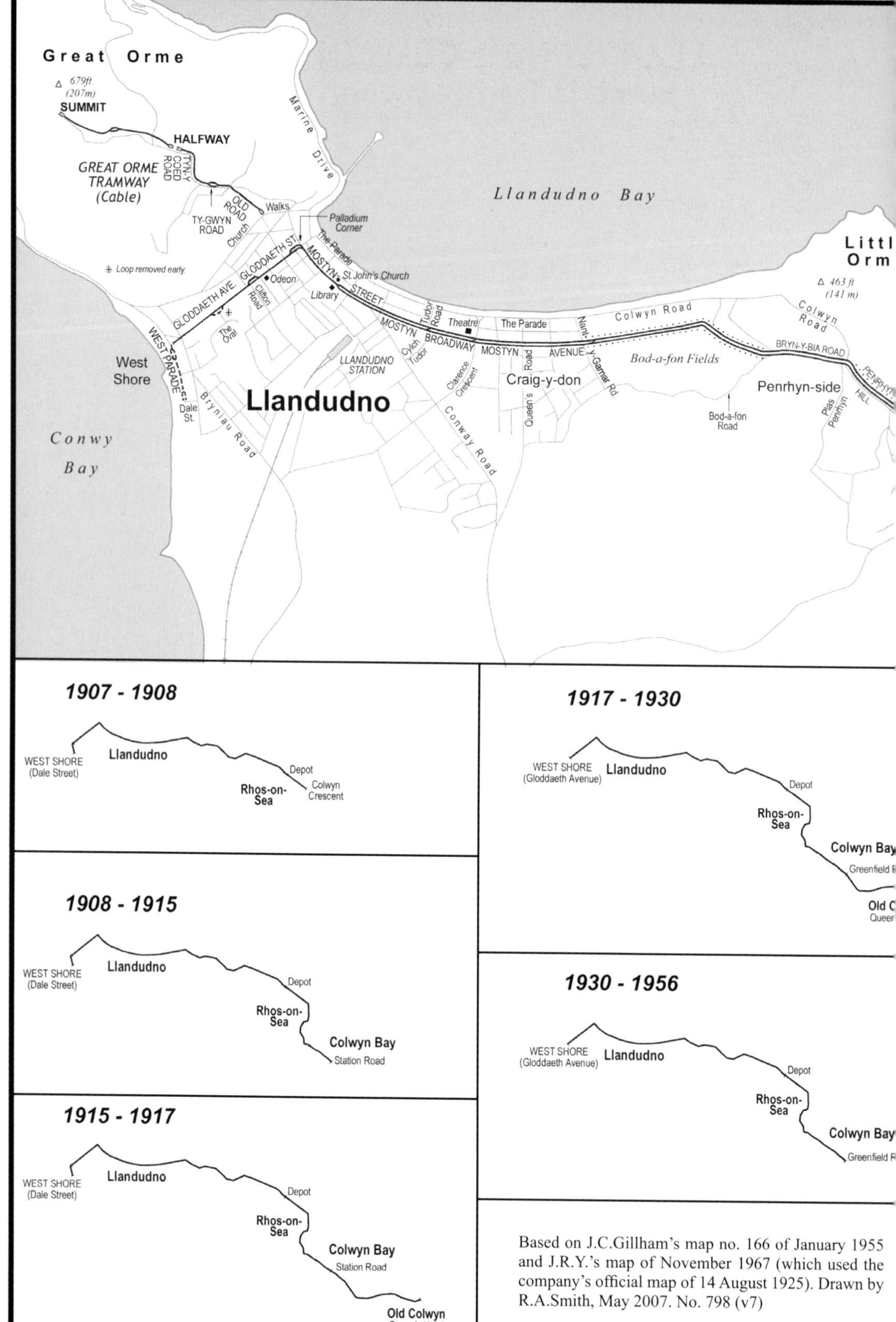

Based on J.C.Gillham's map no. 166 of January 1955 and J.R.Y.'s map of November 1967 (which used the company's official map of 14 August 1925). Drawn by R.A.Smith, May 2007. No. 798 (v7)

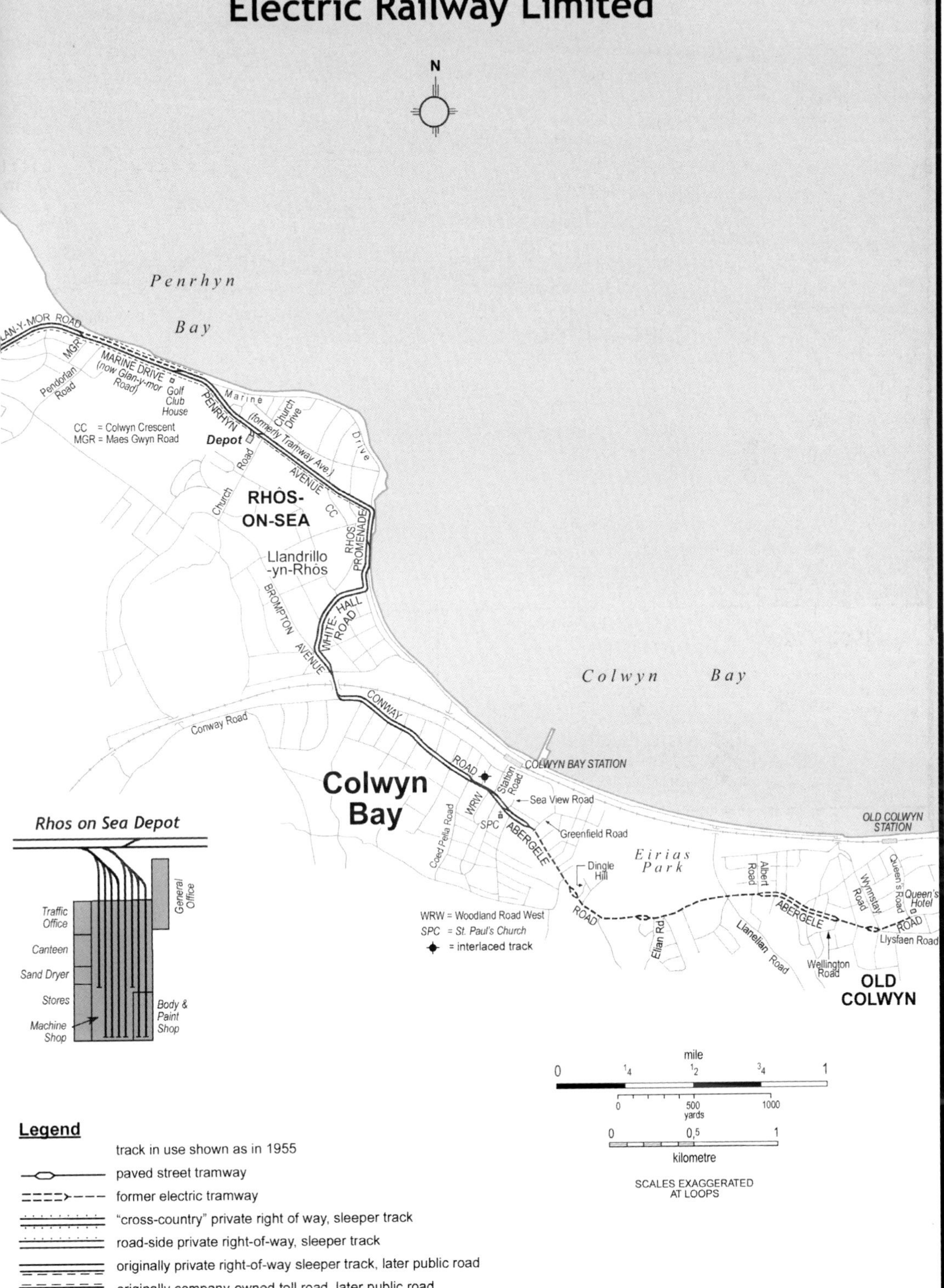
LLANDUDNO & COLWYN BAY
Electric Railway Limited
N
Penrhyn
Bay
Colwyn Bay
RHÔS-
ON-SEA
Llandrillo
-yn-Rhôs
Colwyn
Bay
OLD
COLWYN
Eirias
Park
COLWYN BAY STATION
OLD COLWYN
STATION
MARINE DRIVE
(now Glan-y-mor
Road)
MGR
Pendorlan
Road
Golf
Club
House
CC = Colwyn Crescent
MGR = Maes Gwyn Road
Depot
PENRHYN
AVENUE
(formerly Tramway Ave.)
Marine
Drive
Church
Drive
Church
Road
RHOS
PROMENADE
WHITE- HALL
ROAD
BROMPTON
AVENUE
CONWAY
ROAD
Conway Road
Station
Road
Sea View Road
Greenfield Road
WRW
SPC
Coed Pella Road
ABERGELE
ROAD
Dingle
Hill
Elian Rd
Albert
Road
Llanelian
Road
Wellington
Road
Wynnstay
Road
Queen's Road
Queen's
Hotel
Llysfaen Road
WRW = Woodland Road West
SPC = St. Paul's Church
= interlaced track
Rhos on Sea Depot
Traffic
Office
Canteen
Sand Dryer
Stores
Machine
Shop
General
Office
Body &
Paint
Shop
mile
0
¼
½
¾
1
0
500
yards
1000
0
0,5
1
kilometre
SCALES EXAGGERATED
AT LOOPS
Legend
track in use shown as in 1955
paved street tramway
former electric tramway
"cross-country" private right of way, sleeper track
road-side private right-of-way, sleeper track
originally private right-of-way sleeper track, later public road
originally company-owned toll road, later public road
other roads
railways

HISTORICAL BACKGROUND

The need for a frequent, and direct public transport service between Llandudno and Colwyn Bay came to the fore during the latter part of the nineteenth century, when the two towns were rapidly developing as seaside resorts. Whilst Colwyn Bay was served by a railway station on the North Wales coast main line between Chester and Holyhead, Llandudno, the larger of the two towns, was at the end of a three mile long branch line from the main line at Llandudno Junction. Thus travel between the two towns involved an indirect railway journey with probably a change of train en route.

Proposals were made during the 1890s to construct a direct tramway between the two towns, and this resulted in the granting of a Light Railway Order by the Light Railway Commissioners in 1899. The Llandudno and Colwyn Bay Light Railway Order of 1898 empowered the construction of an 8 mile/12.8km - 3' 6"/1067mm gauge light railway between Deganwy (situated on the Conwy Estuary near Llandudno Junction), via Llandudno, Penrhyn Bay and Rhos on Sea, to Colwyn Bay railway station. Over the next few years, there followed numerous attempts to build the line. All of these failed, until in 1906 the Llandudno and District Electric Tramway Construction Company took over the powers of the 1898 Order and engaged Bruce Peebles, tramway contractors, to build the line. From then on, progress in constructing the line was swift and by the latter half of 1907, the Company was confident in arranging to commence a service over the greater part of the line.

As originally constructed, the tramway, over five miles in length, started at Llandudno West Shore (Dale Street) and finished at Rhos on Sea, near to the depot and adjacent to Rhos seafront. It was entirely single track with several passing loops and outside the built up areas was largely constructed on its own right of way over fields or on unmade roads. At Penrhyn Hill, on the landward side of the Little Orme, a ledge was blasted out of the rock to provide a trackbed and here the trams faced a maximum gradient of 1 in 11.5/8.6%.

The Board of Trade inspection took place on 26th September, and the line opened to the public on Saturday, 19th October 1907.

Two Brush-built single deck cars built for the Canvey Island tramway, but never delivered, were used by Bruce Peebles for test purposes, but these had disappeared by the time of the opening. The initial Llandudno fleet comprised fourteen long, interurban style bogie single deckers, painted in a maroon livery and lettered 'Llandudno & Colwyn Bay'. At first the service was sparse, being to a 30 minute frequency, but this was improved the following month.

Further powers obtained by the company varied the original authorised route from Rhos into Colwyn Bay, and this section was opened for traffic on 7th June 1908, bringing the route mileage to over six miles. The cars terminated in Colwyn Bay in Conway Road at the junction with Station Road, the original plan to run to the station entrance itself being abandoned.

In 1909, the company changed its name to the familiar 'Llandudno and Colwyn Bay Electric Railway Ltd'. Note that the word 'company' was not used in the new title.

Further expansion plans involved an extension of the line beyond Colwyn Bay via Abergele Road to Old Colwyn, and this eventually opened to traffic on 26th March 1915, bringing the route mileage to its maximum of over eight miles. Meanwhile, most of the original route, consisting of single track, was gradually being converted to double track, a programme that was not completed until 1929 when the widening of Conway Road in Colwyn Bay allowed tracks to be doubled here. From then, with two exceptions, double track extended from Mostyn Street in Llandudno to Colwyn Bay town centre. A short section of single track was retained over the railway bridge in Brompton Avenue, and interlaced tracks were laid in a narrow part of Conway Road in Colwyn Bay, between Hawarden Road and Station Road. The West Shore and Old Colwyn sections at the outer ends of the route remained as single track.

The Old Colwyn extension never came up to expectations, and this section was abandoned on 22nd September 1930, the service being taken over by Crosville buses. A short part at the Colwyn Bay end was retained, allowing the eastern terminus to be at the junction with Greenfield

Road. The stretch of track at West Shore, between the western end of Gloddaeth Avenue and Dale Street, which was the nearest the line got to Deganwy, had been formally abandoned some years previously. From the very beginning, this section had never carried any sort of regular service, and had latterly been used by the occasional tram to collect sand, which was used as an aid to braking in slippery conditions. From 1930 the route mileage was 6.5 miles/10.4km, and it remained so for the rest of the line's existence.

The trams now suffered from bus competition, and this would be the case for much of the remaining life of the tramway. The company considered replacement of the trams by trolleybuses, but this was rejected in part because of the punitive costs of lifting the track and re-instating the roads.

Most of the original rolling stock was replaced in the mid-1930s by secondhand trams. A batch of open topped cars from Bournemouth introduced double deckers into the fleet, and the Board of Trade only agreed to their use provided that the wind speed on exposed sections of track did not exceed 50 miles per hour/80.4km/h.

The war years were busy for the tramway. Restrictions on fuel curtailed motorbus competition and passenger use was swelled by the evacuation of Government departments into the area. For the duration, the Inland Revenue had been moved to Llandudno and the Ministry of Food to Rhos.

After the war, several problems began to mount up for the company, despite record numbers of holidaymakers visiting the area. Two relatively modern, but second hand, streamlined double deck cars bought in 1946 proved to be unsuitable for the line. The stretch of track beside the sea at Penrhyn Bay, which had always been susceptible to erosion damage, became a real cause for concern. Storms in January 1952 seriously undermined the Marine Drive coast road, resulting in single line working being introduced between Maesgwyn Road and the Golf House. Crossovers at these points had been inserted following previous damage to the track here in the late 1940s. From early 1952, the seaward track between these points was permanently abandoned. Adding to these problems, the Electricity Board served notice to the company that their charges would greatly increase, to take account of the real cost of maintaining staff to supply the company's power requirements.

In October 1954 the directors of the company announced their intention to replace the trams with buses and to apply for the necessary licences. This was scheduled to take place by the end of 1955, but complications with the granting of the bus service licences and protracted negotiations with the local authorities about the arrangements for road reinstatement delayed the process. Great efforts were made by enthusiasts to save the line, and shares were bought in the company with this in mind. However, this initiative did not bear fruit, and, in January 1956, as if to demonstrate that there was no going back, the company began dismantling the trams not required for the winter service. Thus the last trams ran on Saturday, 24th March 1956.

The 'Red Buses', as the replacement fleet of elderly buses was known, continued to face intense competition from Crosville and in May 1961 the company finally sold its goodwill to its rival.

CONSTRUCTION AND TRIALS

1. The construction of the track was undertaken during 1907 by Bruce Peebles & Co Ltd. This is the Bodafon Fields reserved track looking towards Llandudno with Llandudno Bay on the right. A passing loop and overhead are in course of completion.
(Bruce Peebles/A.W.Brotchie coll.)

→ 2. Car 3 is seen under test on Penrhyn Hill. Note the single trolley pole which was very soon replaced by the double pole arrangement on all this type of car and the lack of wording or crest on the car's side.
(Bruce Peebles/A.W.Brotchie coll.)

→ 3. An end-on view depicts car 3 on test at Penrhyn Hill, before the line was handed over from the contractor to the operating company. (Bruce Peebles/A.W.Brotchie coll.)

4. This view shows the undeveloped nature of the area around Tramway Avenue, looking towards Rhos on Sea from the depot. Note the lattice type traction poles planted on the ground in concrete blocks. (Bruce Peebles/A.W.Brotchie coll.)

5. The initial line ended at Rhos on Sea, near the end of Tramway Avenue which was later renamed Penrhyn Avenue. One of the original cars stands at the terminus which was near Colwyn Crescent. The buildings in the background are situated on Rhos sea front. Note that the car carries the legend 'Llandudno & Colwyn Bay' on its side. (Author's coll.)

WEST SHORE

6. West Shore, where the line terminated, was the least busy of Llandudno's two sea fronts. It was reached via a 2/3rd mile stretch of single track from the town centre, along Gloddaeth Avenue, with one passing loop halfway along at Clifford Street. Looking west, this view shows the end of the line at the junction of Gloddaeth Avenue and West Parade with the seashore in the background. Due to the single track layout, it was not usual to see two cars together at the terminus. On this occasion, car 8 on the left, is working on an enthusiasts' tour for the Light Railway Transport League, whilst car 15 is a normal service car. The date is Saturday, 6th June 1954. (R.J.S.Wiseman)

7. Toastrack car 22 loads passengers at the terminus, which overlooked the Conway (now Conwy) estuary, giving views along the North Wales coast towards Penmaenmawr and Anglesey. The mountains of Snowdonia are visible in the background. (A.D.Packer)

8 Looking east towards Llandudno centre, toastrack car 21 prepares to depart with another load of passengers about to experience a 'fresh air' ride. This busy scene is dated 20th July 1955, during the last summer of the tramway. Note the sign pointing to the West Shore open air Lido. Like the tramway, this is another Llandudno attraction that no longer exists. (Author's coll.)

WEST SHORE: 1920s and 1930s

9. This late 1920s view is of original single deck car 11 at West Shore. The car was renumbered 17 in 1936 and as such it ran until 1955. Note the roof boards with the final destination as 'Colwyn', denoting the extension to Old Colwyn abandoned in 1930. The conductor is securing the front trolley pole before raising the rear one for the next journey. The large circular passenger shelter (which still exists) can be seen through the car's windows. A window bill on the car reads 'Ride beside the seaside – 1/- return'. As well as on the tramway, these tickets were valid between Llandudno and Colwyn Bay on Crosville buses and the LMS railway. They were withdrawn on the outbreak of war and never reinstated. (Author's coll.)

10. Five ex Accrington single deck cars entered service in 1933, still in the Accrington bright red and pale cream livery; they ran like this until about 1936. This is car 4 waiting at West Shore. Three of these cars, including this one, were fitted with the bogies from the 1907 cars that they replaced. (L&CBTS collection/Conwy Archive Service)

11. A rare view of one of the four 1909 built single truck 'Yankee' trams, car 15, at West Shore is from the mid-1930s, shortly before these were withdrawn and replaced by the Bournemouth cars. These single truck trams had a reputation for speed and lively riding. (J.Fozard)

GLODDAETH AVENUE

12. Gloddaeth Avenue is a long, wide street with a median strip. The tramway ran alongside this central strip in the southernmost carriageway. Car 8 proceeds eastwards towards Palladium Corner. The large building visible in the background is the Odeon Cinema (formerly the Astra Theatre), adjacent to the Clifford Street loop. The date is Whit Sunday, 7th June 1954. (R.J.S.Wiseman)

13. Latterly, the only passing loop on the single track section to West Shore was at Clifford Street. Here, car 7 enters the loop from the West Shore direction. The two tracks at the loop were set quite a distance apart, wide enough to enable motorists to park between the tracks, as seen here! (R.J.S.Wiseman)

14. East of Clifford Street, Gloddaeth Avenue becomes Gloddaeth Street. This early view shows an original single deck car, proceeding towards West Shore, passing the site of what was to become the Astra Theatre, built in 1934. In the background is a steamer leaving Llandudno Pier for Liverpool. This was *La Marguerite*, which served Llandudno from 1904 to 1926. (Commercial postcard/Geoff Smith coll.)

PALLADIUM CORNER

15. The busiest point on the system was the corner of Mostyn Street and Gloddaeth Street, known as Palladium Corner, the nearest point on the tram route to the Pier and Llandudno Bay. In the high summer, when every available car was in service, extra cars from Colwyn Bay would terminate here, as well as any late running timetabled cars, which would be turned short by the Palladium Corner inspector in an effort to keep these cars running to time. 'Jumper' conductors were employed (notably Charlie O'Malley) to take fares from the waiting queue and then travel along Mostyn Street, jumping onto an incoming tram to return and repeat the performance. The passing loop here extended around the corner into Mostyn Street. This late 1940s view shows Darwen streamliner car 23 working the local service to Craig y Don, having just reversed. Car 15 has just come round the corner from Mostyn Street with another load of passengers from Colwyn Bay. (Roy Brook/Craig Ollerton/Llandudno Enthusiasts)

16. Accrington car 2 in Gloddaeth Street is seen loading passengers at Palladium Corner in July 1950. This car was one of the two of this type purchased complete with its original Accrington Brush maximum traction trucks, and as such gave a smoother ride than those fitted with trucks from withdrawn cars. The ornate building in the background is the Palladium Cinema, after which this point was commonly known. (J.H.Meredith)

(*lower left*) 17. An early 1930s view depicts toastrack 19, at Palladium Corner. The crew pose at the controls, although the trolley appears to have been turned for the return journey. Note the large route indicator board used on these cars in pre-war years. (Dr H.A.Whitcombe)

18. Car 16, one of the four wheel 'Yankee' trams, built in 1909, stands at Palladium Corner. It is working on the Llandudno local service between West Shore and Craig y Don, a regular turn for these cars. This view dates from around 1930. (Dr H.A.Whitcombe)

Timetable July 1932. *Continued below picture 69.*

Llandudno and Colwyn Bay Electric Railway Ltd.

TIME TABLE.

Llandudno and Colwyn Bay—Week Days.

	am	am	am	am †	am †	am	am	am	am	am	am	am	am	am	am	am	am	am	am	am	am	am	am
Llandudno West Shore	...	...	...	7 15	7 25	...	...	7 35	7 45	...	7 55	8 3	8 8	8 13	8 18	8 23	8 28	8 33	8 38	8 43	8 48	8 53	8 58
Hooson's Corner	...	...	...	7 19	7 29	...	...	7 40	7 50	...	7 59	8 7	8 12	8 17	8 22	8 27	8 32	8 37	8 42	8 47	8 52	8 57	9 2
Queen's Road	...	...	...	7 25	7 35	...	...	7 46	7 56	...	8 6	8 13	8 18	8 23	8 28	8 33	8 38	8 43	8 48	8 53	8 58	9 3	9 8
Penrhynside	...	...	...	7 32	7 42	...	...	7 54	8 4	...	8 13	8 20	8 25	8 30	8 35	8 40	8 45	8 50	8 55	9 0	9 5	9 10	9 15
Rhos-on-Sea	7 10	7 20	7 30	7 42	7 52	8 0	8 5	8 7	8 14	8 18	8 23	8 30	8 35	8 40	8 45	8 50	8 55	9 0	9 5	9 10	9 15	9 20	9 25
Colwyn Bay	7 18	7 28	7 38	7 50	8 0	8 8	8 13	8 16	8 22	8 26	8 33	8 38	8 43	8 48	8 53	8 58	9 3	9 8	9 13	9 18	9 23	9 28	9 33

	am		pm	pm	pm	pm	pm	pm	pm	pm	pm	pm *	pm *	pm *	pm	pm	pm	pm	pm	pm
Llandudno West Shore	9 3	Then every 5 Minutes until	9 38	9 43	9 48	9 53	9 58	10 3	10 8	10 13	10 18	10 23	10 28	10 33	10 38	10 43	10 48	10 53	10 58	11 3
Hooson's Corner	9 7		9 42	9 47	9 52	9 57	10 2	10 7	10 12	10 17	10 22	10 27	10 32	10 37	10 42	10 47	10 52	10 57	11 2	11 7
Queen's Road	9 13		9 48	9 53	9 58	10 3	10 8	10 13	10 18	10 23	10 28	10 33	10 38	10 43	10 48	10 53	10 58	11 3	11 8	11 13
Penrhynside	9 20		9 55	10 0	10 5	10 10	10 15	10 20	10 25	10 30	10 35	10 40	10 45	10 50	10 55	11 0	11 5	11 10	11 15	11 20
Rhos-on-Sea	9 30		10 5	10 10	10 15	10 20	10 25	10 30	10 35	10 40	10 45	10 50	10 55	11 0	11 5	11 10	11 15	11 20	11 25	11 30
Colwyn Bay	9 38		10 13	10 18	10 23	10 28	10 33	10 38	10 43	10 48	10 53	10 58	11 3	11 8	...	...	...	...	...	...

* Subject to slight alteration to meet the requirements of the Llandudno Theatres.

† These Cars connect with the Club Train at Colwyn Bay.

Llandudno and Colwyn Bay—Sundays.

	am	am	am	am	pm	pm	pm	pm	pm	pm	pm	pm		pm	pm	pm	pm	pm	pm	pm
Llandudno West Shore	...	10 30	10 55	11 40	12 10	12 35	12 52	1 6	1 22	1 38	1 54	2 10	Then every 16 Minutes until	8 50	9 6	9 22	9 38	9 54	10 10	10 26
Hooson's Corner	...	10 34	10 59	11 44	12 14	12 39	12 56	1 12	1 28	1 44	2 0	2 16		8 56	9 12	9 28	9 44	10 0	10 16	10 32
Queen's Road	...	10 40	11 5	11 50	12 20	12 45	1 2	1 18	1 34	1 50	2 6	2 22		9 2	9 18	9 34	9 50	10 6	10 22	10 38
Penrhynside	...	10 47	11 12	11 57	12 28	12 55	1 10	1 26	1 42	1 58	2 14	2 30		9 10	9 26	9 42	9 58	10 14	10 30	10 46
Rhos-on-Sea	10 12	10 57	11 22	12 7	12 36	1 5	1 20	1 36	1 52	2 8	2 24	2 40		9 20	9 36	9 52	10 8	10 24	10 40	10 56
Colwyn Bay	10 20	11 5	11 30	12 15	12 45	1 15	1 30	1 46	2 2	2 18	2 34	2 50		9 30	9 46	10 2	10 18	10 34	10 50	...

19. Bournemouth car 7 sets off from Palladium Corner to turn into Mostyn Street, as toastrack car 21 makes the turn in the opposite direction. The loop only extended for a few yards into Mostyn Street, before reverting to single track. Drivers had to take care to ensure that the single track was not occupied by an oncoming car - otherwise an unscheduled reversal back around the corner would ensue! (R.F.Mack)

20. Car 12 arrives at Palladium Corner and prepares to make the turn into Gloddaeth Street. The squeal from the tram wheels when making this manoeuvre was a feature of life here until the trams ceased in 1956. The top deck passengers are already standing up in anticipation of alighting round the corner. (R.J.S.Wiseman)

MOSTYN STREET AND MOSTYN BROADWAY

21. Mostyn Street is Llandudno's main shopping street. In this view, dated Whit Sunday 1954, car 6 has entered the loop prior to turning left into Gloddaeth Street with the mass of the Great Orme in the background. A well laden double deck car can be seen on the left ready to depart from Palladium Corner towards Colwyn Bay. (R.J.S.Wiseman)

I 7414

LLANDUDNO & COLWYN BAY ELECTRIC RLY. LTD.

Stage		Stage
1		6
2		5
3	10	4
4		3
5		2
6		1

Ticket is to be punched in the section to which Passen... to tra-vel, and mu... Issued su...ect to the Bye-laws.

AUTOTICKETS LTD. BIRKENHEAD

22. This is a scene from the early days of the tramway. Car 9 proceeds north along Edwardian Mostyn Street at its junction with Lloyd Street. The building on the left on the corner of Lloyd Street was later replaced by a bank. (Commercial Postcard/Geoff Smith coll.)

23. Mostyn Street in the late 1930s is seen here, again showing the junction with Lloyd Street with the bank on the left. An ex Accrington car proceeds south.
(Commercial Postcard/Geoff Smith coll.)

35. Looking back towards Craig y Don, car 8 is seen on the reserved track, which at this point ran parallel with Llandudno Bay. This view was taken in September 1955, at the end of the final summer season of the tramway. (J.B.Snell)

36. The reserved track took trams near the Little Orme, passing the district of Craigside, where an intermediate stop was provided. Car 7 turns towards Craigside as it begins to climb towards Penrhyn Hill on 7th June 1954. (R.J.S.Wiseman)

37. Rather battered, car 10 pauses at the Craigside stop in 1947. A waiting shelter, said to be constructed from the body parts of withdrawn trams, was provided and this was near the stile over the fence, on the left. (A.E.Old)

Where does the tram go?

Destination signs on the trams were generally reversible boards shown at each end of the tram as appropriate. Some types of car were fitted with more detailed information as follows.

Original bogie cars 1 to 14
Until 1930, when the Old Colwyn section was abandoned, these cars carried long wooden boards along the roof-line lettered :-
LLANDUDNO PENRHYN HILL for The Little Orme and Gloddaeth Woods PENRHYN BAY RHOS on SEA COLWYN BAY & COLWYN for Fairy Glen and Penmaen Head

From 1930, these boards were altered to read :
LLANDUDNO PENRHYN HILL LITTLE ORME PENRYHN BAY RHOS on SEA Swimming Pool & COLWYN BAY

These were also carried by the Accrington and Bournemouth cars.

The boards were removed during the Second World War.

The Bournemouth cars had signs at each end, behind the drivers vestibule, showing a pointing hand and 'To LLANDUDNO' or 'To COLWYN BAY' as appropriate. These were removed in wartime but reinstated afterwards. The Darwen cars also carried these until they were confined to working in Colwyn Bay, when paper stickers where affixed over the central entrance showing 'RHOS ON SEA' and 'COLWYN BAY'.

In 1952, paper stickers were affixed above the side windows of the Accrington and Bournemouth cars showing:

LLANDUDNO PIER LITTLE ORME PENRHYN BAY RHOS on SEA COLWYN BAY

In addition, the toastrack cars had yellow stickers low down on their front dashes showing LLANDUDNO PIER, or COLWYN BAY on the appropriate end of each car.

38. With Llandudno Bay in the background, this mid 1930s view shows single truck 'Yankee' car 16 continuing the climb from Craigside, shortly before these cars were taken out of service. Note the small fleet numbers used on this type of tram, necessitated by the small space above the headlight. Toastrack 22 also carried this style of number for a period in the 1940s. (W.J.Haynes/D. Voice/Tramway and Light Railway Society)

39. Looking down on the upper end of the reserved track section, car 13 can be seen climbing from Craigside in June 1954, illustrating the superb views of Llandudno Bay and the Great Orme that could be seen from the trams. (R.J.S.Wiseman)

BRYN Y BIA ROAD

40. At the top end of the Bodafon Fields section, the track entered Bryn y Bia Road. Here car 12 is seen about to emerge onto the road at this point. Note the official L&CBER board warning of the private right of way. In 1948, it was a three-halfpenny fare to Craig y Don from the tram stop seen on the left, at that time the only such fare on the whole route. (Roy Brook)

41. Bryn y Bia Road led to the top of Penrhyn Hill and was little more than a country lane. In the first days of the tramway car 14 is seen leaving the original loop in the single track. (Commercial postcard/Geoff Smith coll.)

42. By contrast to the previous view, here is car 9 in Bryn y Bia Road in 1952, showing the rural nature of the area. Note that the left hand (Llandudno bound) track was placed very close to the edge of the road. (R.J.S.Wiseman)

43. At the top of Penrhyn Hill, behind the Little Orme, the trams crossed the main Llandudno Road to descend towards Rhos and Colwyn Bay. This early view shows a car, having emerged from Bryn y Bia Road, crossing to descend Penrhyn Hill on the reserved track. At this time the modern road, had not been built. (Commercial Postcard/Geoff Smith coll.)

PENRHYN HILL

44. The tramway negotiated Penrhyn Hill on a ledge blasted out of the hillside and at its steepest point was a gradient of 1 in 11. This early view shows car 2 ascending the hill showing the original single-track formation. (Author's coll.)

45. Car 10 is seen climbing to the top of the hill. The main Llandudno Road, which ran parallel with the tramway but at a slightly lower level, crossed the tramway at the summit, where the prominent 'Welcome to Llandudno' sign is situated. (J.B.Snell)

46. This 1920s view shows the three roads at Penrhyn Hill. The original lane is at the lowest level. Beside the tramway is the new motor road, which was built in 1921. A 'Yankee' four wheel car ascends the hill. (Commercial postcard/Geoff Smith coll.)

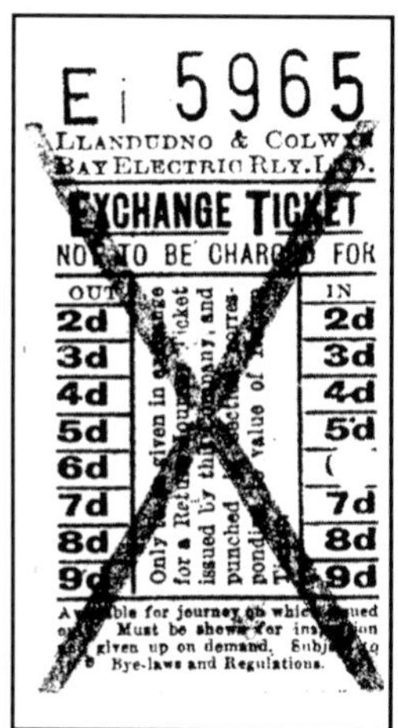

Ei 5965

LLANDUDNO & COLW
AY ELECTRIC RLY. L

CHANGE TIC ET

NO O BE CHAR FOR

OUT		IN
2d		2d
3d		3d
4d		4d
5d		5d
6d		(
7d		7d
8d		8d
9		9d

Only given in for a Ret issued by th punched pondi value of

A ble for journey on whi ued
Must be shewn for ins ion
given up on demand. Subj o
Bye-laws and Regulations.

47. Car 8 powers up the steepest part of the hill in August 1955, whilst the top deck passengers enjoy the views that would not be available from the following year. The replacement buses had, of course to use the lower road with all the other traffic. (A.B.Cross/C.Barker coll.)

48. A view of car 12 descending the hill, shows the magnificent panorama of Rhos and Colwyn Bay in the background, and the traffic on the main road. The track crossing the line behind the car led to one of the quarry workings around the Little Orme, which was a source of ballast for the tramway. The Little Orme Café can be seen to the left of the road junction in the background. (R.J.S.Wiseman)

49. Passengers brave the winter air on the upper deck of car 6 as it begins the climb of Penrhyn Hill on 25th January 1947. The difference in level between the tramway and the 1921 motor road is evident in this view. This was the period of post war austerity, as demonstrated by the exhortation on the car's fender - 'Save Fuel Save Light'. (A.E.Old)

SH 7708

LLANDUDNO & COLWYN BAY ELECTRIC RLY. LTD.

Stage	5d	Stage
1	Ticket is to be punched in the section to which Passenger is entitled to travel, and must be shown on demand. Issued subject to the Bye-Laws.	5
2		4
3		3
4		2
5		1

AUTO-TICKETS LIMITED, BIRKENHEAD

GLAN Y MOR ROAD

50. The tram stop at the bottom of Penrhyn Hill was at the Little Orme Café. Here, the route ran into Glan y Mor Road on a roadside grassed reservation. Car 18, showing signs of extensive body sag, is standing at the stop, which was provided with a shelter and nameboard 'Little Orme Café'. The shelter is hidden by the tram. This car received a full repaint in the late 1940s. (Roy Brook)

LR 7811

LLANDUDNO & COLWYN BAY ELECTRIC RLY. LTD.

STAGE	1d	STAGE
1	Ticket is to be punched in the section to which Passenger is entitled to travel, must be shown on demand. Issued subject to the Bye-laws.	12
2		11
3		10
4		9
5		8
6		7
7		6
8		5
9		4
10		3
11		2
12		1

AUTO-TICKETS LTD. BIRKENHEAD

51. Looking in the opposite direction to the previous view, car 11 draws up to the Little Orme Café stop to pick up this family party in September 1955. The man on the right is the noted historian of North Wales narrow gauge railways, James I.C.Boyd. (J.B.Snell)

52. At Whitsuntide 1954, the Light Railway Transport League held their annual conference at Llandudno, and the programme included an extensive private tour of the tramway. Bad weather on the day precluded the use of the hoped for toastrack car, but brighter weather in the late afternoon allowed the party to have a short trip from the depot to the foot of Penrhyn Hill in car 21. The car is about to reverse on the crossover near the end of Glan y Mor Road. (R.J.S.Wiseman)

53. Further east along Glan y Mor Road, the line curved towards Penrhyn Bay. This was an unadopted and unsurfaced road and its condition is apparent in this view showing Accrington car 5. In the background is the St Paul's Road stop, where a small wooden passenger shelter with nameboard was provided. The tram is passing the home of the company General Manager, W.G.Hamilton. (J.B.Snell)

54. Looking towards Rhos, this is a view of the eastern part of Glan y Mor Road, where it curves towards the sea at Penrhyn Bay. Cars 8 and 4 pass near the Benarth Road stop, where, in the right background, another shelter with nameboard was provided. Note the original lattice traction poles still in situ. Most of these were replaced around 1953 by secondhand poles from Stockport. (R.F.Mack)

55. Looking west along Glan y Mor Road, car 4 waits for car 14 to pass before it uses the crossover just west of the Maesgwyn Road stop. Severe erosion of the foundations of the seaward track from here to the Golf House forced the tramway to adopt single line working from 1952. This is the last day of the trams, and several passengers can be seen standing up on the top deck of car 14 taking photographs. (R.J.S.Wiseman)

PENRHYN BAY

56. Glan y Mor Road led to Penrhyn Bay, where the line ran alongside the sea. This delightful mid-summer scene, near Maesgwyn Road tram stop looking towards Rhos on Sea, shows car 8 (left) about to pass car 7. The date is 21st June 1945, during the first weeks of peace in Europe and the scene was captured at 9.05pm that evening, thanks to the extended daylight achieved with Double British Summer Time. Full double line operation is in force and the original lattice traction poles are evident. (E.C.Haywood)

57. This is Maesgwyn Road tram stop with its wooden shelter visible just behind car 17, which is working towards Colwyn Bay on the landward track. The severity of the damage to the seaward track is evident, and despite all efforts to rectify the situation, after 1952 this track was abandoned and the single line working became permanent. The date is 19th March 1954. (J.B.Snell)

58. In 1954, car 7 heads towards Llandudno at Maesgwyn Road, and from this angle the car appears to be very close to the road edge. Note the van following the tram - it must have been a bumpy ride! (J.B.Snell)

59. Extensive reconstruction work of the sea wall took place during 1954/55, resulting in the scene seen here between Maesgwyn Road and the Golf House. Note that the double track was not re-instated, and the abandoned second track has virtually disappeared. Car 3 proceeds towards Colwyn Bay on a damp and misty 24th March 1956, the last day of tramway operation. The following day, the company's buses would be bumping over this road. (R.J.S.Wiseman)

60. The latter day single track section extended to the Golf House Toll Gate, where the double track resumed. Another last day photograph shows car 14 negotiating the crossover to regain the seaward track. The stub end of this can just be seen in the foreground before the tracks disappear under tarmac. On the extreme left is the new sea wall and promenade. The Vauxhall on the right is in the Golf Club car park. This section of road, as far as Orme Point, was owned by the tram company, and a toll was charged for other traffic. The original land owner allowed the tram tracks to be laid over his land in 1907, and then introduced tolls for other classes of traffic (including pedestrians) in 1908. The land was taken over by the tram company in 1911, and it continued to collect tolls (latterly for vehicles only) until the L&CBER company was liquidated in 1963. Large boards warning of the toll, and setting out the various charges for each class of vehicle, were displayed at Orme Point, near the end of Marine Drive. (R.J.S.Wiseman)

PENRHYN AVENUE AND THE DEPOT

61. At Orme Point, shortly after the tramway had crossed the Llandudno - Colwyn Bay boundary (and into Denbighshire from Caernarvonshire), the tramway turned inland into Penrhyn Avenue. Originally this road was named Tramway Avenue, and the whole area was undeveloped, being known locally as 'Klondyke' (see photograph 4). Car 17 pauses at Orme Point stop on 13th May 1955. Note the typical cast iron tram stop on the right. These were provided by Colwyn Bay Council and incorporated the council crest. (A.D.Packer/C.Barker coll.)

62. Standing astride the crossover outside the depot in July 1950, car 14 awaits a relief crew. The upper deck passengers, anxious to enjoy the delights of Colwyn Bay or Rhos, look towards the depot for the crew to appear and the journey resume. (J.H.Meredith)

63. The depot entrance is seen here in the later years of the tramway. Trams could only enter or leave the depot in the Llandudno direction, and a reverse was necessary in Penrhyn Avenue for trams taking up or finishing service from the Colwyn Bay end of the line. This track arrangement meant that the cars could never be turned, and each car therefore had a 'Llandudno' end and a 'Colwyn Bay' end. Whilst the depot overhead extended as far as the wires in Penrhyn Avenue, there were no frogs here and cars needed to have their trolley poles manually changed. The procedure was that the cars were 'trolleyed' in and out of the depot, the conductor holding the trolley rope and walking beside the car. The cars always left the depot building trolley first, and the trolley was then swung once into the yard. Car 8 is seen here in the depot gateway. (J.Fozard)

64. This is the depot building immediately before the opening of the line. There were eight tracks inside the shed, enough to house the initial fleet of fourteen cars and provide repair facilities. Ten of the new cars are seen here. Looking from the left, cars 5, 1, 3, 10, 11 13, 12, 14 can be identified. The building survived until 2006, when it was demolished and the site redeveloped for housing. (A.W.Brotchie coll.)

→ 65. An interesting photograph showing red and cream liveried Darwen car 24 arriving at the depot in August 1946, after its journey by road from Lancashire. This vehicle eventually entered service as car 23 in April 1948. Note the rough surface of the depot yard. The figure in the hat, standing to the right of the car, is thought to be W.G.Hamilton, the General Manager. (L&CBTS coll./Conwy Archive Service)

→ 66. This 1952 view of car 13 looks towards Rhos along Penrhyn Avenue and shows that the original lattice type traction poles are still in use. Compare this scene with that shown in photograph 4, which shows the same area as it was when the tramway opened in 1907. (R.J.S.Wiseman)

CLARES for FASHIONS
13

67. Church Road was the main stopping point in Penrhyn Avenue. Here passengers are seen alighting from car 5 on 25th September 1955. Note the closeness of the pavement to the Llandudno bound track. An interesting comparison can be made with the previous photograph, which shows that the lattice tram poles have been replaced with conventional ones. (R.J.S.Wiseman)

68. At the Rhos end of Penrhyn Avenue, the tramway turned right onto the sea front. Here, car 12 has just turned off the promenade into Penrhyn Avenue, flanked by a choice selection of 1950s family cars. Parked on the left, is a well laden Ford Prefect and a Triumph Mayflower. The motorist anxious at all costs to get ahead of the tram is driving a Hillman Minx. (J.Fozard)

RHOS ON SEA

69. An early view features original car 10 on Rhos sea front, about to turn left into Penrhyn Avenue. Note that originally the destination board was carried in the centre window at the end of the car. (Commercial postcard/Author's coll.)

Colwyn Bay and Llandudno—Week Days

	am	am	am	am	am	am	am	am	am	am	am	am	am	am	am	am	am	am	am	am	am	am	am
Colwyn Bay	...	...	...	...	7 20	...	7 30	...	7 40	...	7 50	...	8 3	8 8	8 13	8 18	8 23	8 28	8 33	8 38	8 43	8 48	8 53
Rhos-on-Sea	...	...	...	...	7 28	...	7 38	...	7 48	...	7 58	...	8 11	8 16	8 21	8 26	8 31	8 36	8 41	8 46	8 51	8 56	9 1
Penrhynside	6 56	7 6	7 16	7 26	7 38	7 45	7 48	7 56	8 0	8 4	8 9	8 15	8 21	8 26	8 31	8 36	8 41	8 46	8 51	8 56	9 1	9 6	9 11
Queen's Road ...	7 3	7 13	7 23	7 33	7 45	7 52	7 56	8 3	8 7	8 11	8 16	8 22	8 28	8 33	8 38	8 43	8 48	8 53	8 58	9 3	9 8	9 13	9 18
Hooson's Corner	7 9	7 19	7 29	7 39	7 51	7 58	8 4	8 9	8 12	8 17	8 22	8 29	8 34	8 39	8 44	8 49	8 54	8 59	9 4	9 9	9 14	9 19	9 24
Llandudno West Shore ...	7 13	7 23	7 33	7 43	7 55	8 2	8 8	8 13	8 16	8 23	8 28	8 33	8 38	8 43	8 48	8 53	8 58	9 3	9 8	9 13	9 18	9 23	9 28

	am		pm	pm	pm	pm	pm	pm	pm	pm	pm	pm	pm	pm	pm	pm	pm	pm	pm	pm
Colwyn Bay	8 58	Then every 5 Minutes until	9 43	9 48	9 53	9 58	10 3	10 8	10 13	10 18	10 23	10 28	10 33	10 38	10 43	10 48	10 53	10 58	11 3	11 8
Rhos-on-Sea	9 6		9 51	9 56	10 1	10 6	10 11	10 16	10 21	10 26	10 31	10 36	10 41	10 46	10 51	10 56	11 1	11 6	11 11	11 16
Penrhynside	9 16		10 1	10 6	10 11	10 16	10 21	10 26	10 31	10 36	10 41	10 46	...	...	...	...	...	...	...	...
Queen's Road ...	9 23		10 8	10 13	10 18	10 23	10 28	10 33	10 38	10 43	10 48	10 53	...	...	...	...	...	...	...	...
Hooson's Corner	9 29		10 14	10 19	10 24	10 29	10 34	10 39	10 44	10 49	10 54	10 59	...	...	...	...	...	...	...	...
Llandudno West Shore ...	9 33		10 18	10 23	10 28	10 33	10 38	10 43	10 48	10 53	10 58	11 3	...	...	...	...	...	...	...	...

Colwyn Bay and Llandudno—Sundays

	am	am	am	am	pm	pm	pm	pm	pm	pm		pm	pm	pm	pm	pm	pm	pm	pm	pm	pm
Colwyn Bay	...	10 20	11 5	11 30	...	12 15	...	12 46	...	1 16	Then every 16 Minutes until	8 28	8 44	9 0	9 16	9 32	9 48	10 4	10 20	10 36	10 50
Rhos-on-Sea	...	10 28	11 13	11 38	...	12 25	...	12 54	...	1 26		8 38	8 54	9 10	9 26	9 42	9 58	10 14	10 30	10 46	11 0
Penrhynside	10 13	10 38	11 23	11 48	12 17	12 35	12 48	1 4	1 20	1 36		8 48	9 4	9 20	9 36	9 52	10 8	...	...	...	...
Queen's Road ...	10 20	10 45	11 30	11 55	12 24	12 41	12 55	1 11	1 26	1 42		8 54	9 10	9 26	9 42	9 58	10 14	...	...	...	...
Hooson's Corner	10 26	10 51	11 36	12 1	12 30	12 47	1 1	1 17	1 32	1 48		9 0	9 16	9 32	9 48	10 4	10 20	...	...	...	...
Llandudno West Shore ...	10 30	10 55	11 40	12 5	12 34	12 51	1 5	1 21	1 36	1 52		9 4	9 20	9 36	9 52	10 8	10 24	...	...	...	...

This Service will be accelerated during the Summer Months.

The Company will endeavour to conform to the above Time Table, but will not hold themselves responsible for any delay or inconvenience caused by unforeseen circumstances.

W. G. HAMILTON, A.M.I.E.E.,
General Manager.

July, 1932.

5166 Herbert Tomkinson (1929) Ltd. Printers, Colwyn Bay.

70. Car 10 is seen again in this 1920s high level view of Rhos promenade. The car has been painted in the overall grey livery introduced on these cars during the First World War. Some of these cars retained this colour until the green and cream livery was introduced in the early 1930s. It is also believed that some cars were painted overall grey during, or just after, the Second World War. Rhos pier is prominent in the background. (L&CBTS coll./Conwy Archive Service)

→ 71. This is a pre-war view of car 6 at the busy stop on the sea front opposite the end of Rhos Road, known as the 'Cayley Arms' stop. Note the white coated driver and the wooden route board above the lower deck windows, a feature discontinued on the outbreak of war. The 'pointing hand' sign is also visible behind the driver's vestibule. (Author's coll.)

→ 72. Seen at the same point as in the previous view, car 1 is at Rhos promenade. Note that Rhos Pier has disappeared. This structure, which was a secondhand purchase from Douglas, Isle of Man, was dismantled in 1954, after part of it was removed during the Second World War for security reasons. (J.Fozard)

MODERN STORE
LLANDUDNO
NIGHTLY
AT 8-15
THE "FOL-DE-ROLS"
LLANDUDNO • PENRHYNHILL
PENRHYN BAY
COLWYN BAY
TO COLWYN BAY
ALMOND CRISPS 
ALMOND CRISPS
LITTLE ORME
PENRHYN BAY
RHOS-ON-SEA
COLWYN BAY

73. The sun tries to penetrate the clouds as toastrack 22 trundles along Rhos promenade, together with a mix of 1950s cars. The increase in private motoring at this time, with the resultant loss of tramway patronage, was a factor in the decision to close the line. (Author's coll.)

74. The short run along the sea front ended at Cayley Promenade, where the cars turned onto the elevated section of the promenade before turning inland at the Mount Stewart Hotel. Original car 1, having come from Colwyn Bay, is about to turn from Cayley Promenade onto the sea front. Note the horse trough on the left, a feature that still exists today. (Commercial postcard/Geoff Smith coll.)

75. Looking in the opposite direction to the previous photograph, car 8 is about to turn onto the seafront at Cayley Promenade. Rhos pier is evident in the distance in this view dated 7th July 1949. (E.C.Haywood)

76. A 1920s view of Cayley Promenade looking towards Rhos, shows the single track layout in place at this time. Toastrack car 20, Llandudno bound, is seen at the passing loop here. The preceding loop was at the Brompton Road end of Whitehall Road and the next loop was at the Cayley Arms on Rhos seafront. Car 20 has the original net type lifeguard, as described in the caption to photograph 107. (Commercial postcard/Geoff Smith coll.)

WHITEHALL ROAD AND BROMPTON AVENUE

77. Looking from Whitehall Road directly towards the sea, car 4 is about to turn into Cayley Promenade near the end of the tramway's last summer season, September 1955. (R.J.S.Wiseman)

78. Car 11 is seen on 13th April 1952 in Whitehall Road outside the Mount Stewart Hotel, having just turned off Cayley Promenade. (R.J.S.Wiseman)

79. At the other end of Whitehall Road is Five Ways junction. Here, bound for Colwyn Bay, car 12 is about to turn into Brompton Road. On the traction pole in the left background is a cast iron Colwyn Bay style bus stop and beneath this is an older type tram stop plate. (C.Carter)

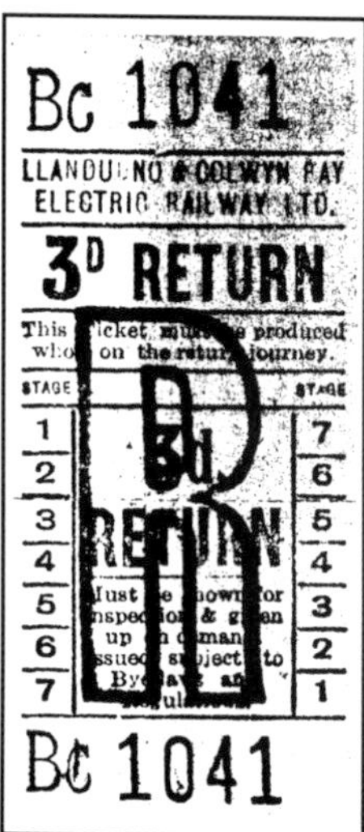

Bc 1041

LLANDUDNO & COLWYN BAY
ELECTRIC RAILWAY LTD.

3D RETURN

This ticket must be produced
when on the return journey.

STAGE		STAGE
1	3d	7
2		6
3	RETURN	5
4		4
5	Must be shown for inspection & given	3
6	up on demand issued subject to	2
7	Bye-laws and Regulations.	1

Bc 1041

80. This is an early view of the tramway in Brompton Road, at the junction with Llanerch Road. The original track layout included a loop in the single track at this point, where the tram in view is presumably waiting before resuming its journey towards Llandudno. Even this close to Colwyn Bay, the area was very undeveloped when the tramway was established. The hill in the background, Bryn Euryn (height 959 feet/292 metres), is a prominent feature overlooking Colwyn Bay. (Commercial postcard/Geoff Smith coll.)

IF 2524

LLANDUDNO & COLWYN BAY ELECTRIC RLY. LTD.

Stage	4d	Stage
1	Ticket is to be punched in the section to which Passenger is entitled to travel, and must be shown on demand. Issued subject to the Bye Laws.	6
2		5
3		4
4		3
5		2
6		1

AUTO-TICKETS LIMITED. BIRKENHEAD

81. Looking along Brompton Road from Llanerch Road, this 1954 view, shows the suburban development of the area. Car 13 is in almost the same position as the early single deck car seen in the previous photograph, albeit travelling in the opposite direction. Five Ways junction is in the background. (R.J.S.Wiseman)

82. Just east of Llanerch Road, Brompton Road turned sharply south to cross the four tracked Crewe to Holyhead railway line. The single tram track was retained across the bridge throughout the life of the tramway. At the other side, the trams turned sharp left into Conway Road, which was then the A55 trunk road along the North Wales coast. Car 6 turns onto the railway bridge from Conway Road showing the double track reverting to single across the span, as two differently styled Vauxhall cars come past in the opposite direction. Today, this area has completely changed, and the line of Brompton Road has been moved slightly west, incorporating a junction with the approach roads to the A55 North Wales Expressway, which now passes under here, together with the railway. (J.Fozard)

COLWYN BAY

83. For the final run into Colwyn Bay, the trams had to deal with the busy traffic, especially heavy in summer, along Conway Road. Outside the Odeon cinema, at the top of Marine Road, there is a battle for road space between car 3 and a Barnsley registered Ford Pilot towing a caravan. Marine Road, as its name implies, runs down to the promenade, passing under the railway en route. (R.J.S.Wiseman)

84. Even in the 1950s, motorists using the A55 road must have been amazed at the sight of a toastrack tram trundling down the road. Outside the Council offices, with the spire of St John's Methodist Church in the background, car 21 pauses at the stop causing traffic to build up behind. The conductor is assisting an elderly lady to negotiate the car step but is she getting on or off? (Author's coll.)

85. The tramway now entered a narrow part of Conway Road in the centre of Colwyn Bay; this stretch between Hawarden Road and Station Road had interlaced track as seen here. A toastrack car is about to leave this section on its way to Llandudno. Hawarden Road is on the left. (H.B. Priestley/National Tramway Muneum)

86. In contrast to the previous photograph, this is the same scene before 1915. The last loop before the Station Road terminus was in this section of Conway Road, and car 13 is seen here just having left the terminus which is in the background. The interlaced track was installed here during the track doubling programme in the late 1920's. (Commercial postcard/Geoff Smith coll.)

87. The original tram terminus at Colwyn Bay was at the top of Station Road. This pre-1915 view, looking along Conway Road, shows car 12 at the terminus before the line was extended to Old Colwyn. (Commercial postcard/ Geoff Smith coll.)

→ 88. Although the Old Colwyn extension from Colwyn Bay was abandoned in 1930, the opportunity was taken to retain the first portion of this in Colwyn Bay town centre to create a new terminus at the top of Greenfield Road. In summer, this section of Conway Road, passing St Paul's Church, could be very congested. There was a crossover here to allow cars to turn back before the terminus. This scene shows toastrack 21, being followed by the inevitable Crosville Leyland bus, which is operating on the route from Llandudno to Rhyl. The bus is passing the crossover in the track. In the background is the site of the original tram terminus, behind the AEC tanker. Two very well laden vehicles are going in the opposite direction. Note that the tram stop on the left displays an additional sign. This reads 'Trams start here for Rhos on Sea, Penrhyn Bay, Craig y Don, Llandudno'. (D.A.Jones/London Trolleybus Preservation Society)

→ 89. Looking in the opposite direction to the previous photograph, car 6 is passing the St Paul's Parish Church stop on the final part of its journey from Llandudno. Parked in the distance is a British Railways Karrier parcel van, of the type used on the Passengers' Luggage in Advance service mentioned in this book's introduction. (J.Fozard)

WOOLWORTH
TRAM STOP
COLWYN BAY
COLWYN BAY

UNION CHURCH
UNION CHURCH
COALITE

90. Accrington car 5 approaches the top of Greenfield Road and is about to pass onto the single track terminal stub, where the passengers will alight. In the distance can be seen one of British Railways' battery electric 'mechanical horse' vehicles. (D.A.Jones/London Trolleybus Preservation Society)

91. Car 7 is seen having just arrived at the terminus. As passengers alight onto the road at the rear, those who have been waiting here start to board at the other end. On the left, but hidden behind the tram, is the café which was used by the crews to replenish their cans of tea. (J.Fozard)

92. This is Colwyn Bay terminus looking east, showing car 8 working the local service to Penrhyn Avenue (Church Road) only. In the 1950s, the basic winter service was a 30 minute frequency, increased to 15 minutes between these points by the operation of these journeys. The date is April 1955. (J.B.Snell)

OLD COLWYN

93. Like the original tramway, the Old Colwyn extension along Abergele Road was single throughout with passing loops, although the loop in Old Colwyn village itself was rather enlongated, giving the impression of double track. Car 8 heads west towards Colwyn Bay in this view of Abergele Road at the Plough Inn. At the dip in the distance, there was a bridge over the Colwyn Brook. The distinctive buildings on the left still survive as do many of those on the right. (Commercial postcard/Geoff Smith coll.)

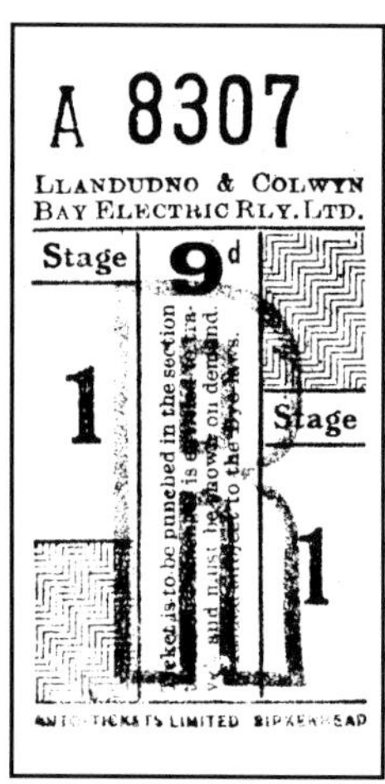

94. Further east in Old Colwyn village, this car is descending from the terminus. The porch doorway of the Ship Inn is on the extreme right. This is another scene that can be easily recognised today. (Commercial postcard/Geoff Smith coll.)

95. The tramway climbed towards the Penmaen Head promontory and terminated beyond the Llysfaen Road junction at the Queens Hotel situated at the top of Queens Road. This is the only known view of a tram at the terminus and is looking east showing the end of the wiring. (Author's coll.)

LOCAL STREAMLINERS

96. 'She'll be comin' round the mountain…' - One of the more interesting aspects of the tramway's operations between 1948 and 1953 was the use of the ex Darwen streamlined cars. These two cars were barred by the Ministry of Transport from carrying passengers over the exposed sections around the Little Orme, and were thus confined to running on the local service at each end of the line. Car 24 is seen nearing the summit of Penrhyn Hill, on its lonely trek to the end of the reserved track at Craig y Don, where it will take up the shuttle service from there into Llandudno. The normal practice was for car 23 to work the Llandudno local during the day then return to depot. Car 24 on the Colwyn Bay local would then run over to Llandudno at teatime and run there until the late evening. (J.S.Webb/National Tramway Museum)

97. In rural surroundings, car 24 is seen negotiating the crossover at Nant y Gamar Road, before travelling back to Llandudno. (L&CBTS coll./Conwy Archive Service)

98. The Llandudno local service commenced from the shelter at the end of the reserved track at Nant y Gamar Road. Here, in 1948, car 23 picks up passengers as Accrington car 1 passes by en route to Colwyn Bay. Note that the Darwen car is showing the destination 'West Shore'. Car 23, the normal choice for the Llandudno local, had the unique destination displays 'West Shore' and 'Nant y Gamar'. Car 24 could only show 'Llandudndo' when working at this end of the line. The destination displays on these cars were not changed once the car had left the depot. (Author's coll.)

99. Car 23 is seen again at the Craig y Don end of Bodafon Fields (Nant y Gamar Road), where the Llandudno local picks up passengers at the shelter provided here. Inspector Fred Shenton, also seen in photograph 15, supervises the proceedings. He emigrated to Canada in the early 1950s. (Roy Brook)

100. The condition of the track in Llandudno did not prove entirely suitable to the operation of these cars, damage being caused to the truck and air brake fittings. Trips beyond Palladium Corner to West Shore were soon curtailed and continued problems with operation in Llandudno led to these cars being confined to Colwyn Bay by the early 1950s. This is car 23 in April 1948, just days after entering service, seen in Mostyn Street near North Western Gardens and Vaughan Street en route for Craig y Don. (A.E.Old)

101. This is a lovely portrait of car 24 at the Colwyn Bay terminus, having arrived from Penrhyn Avenue. The conductor has just unfastened the trolley rope before turning the trolley pole. Trolley ropes were not used in Darwen, so the trolley rope fastening was an L&CBER fitment. In hours of darkness, the conductor would also need to open the driver's door to gain access to the low level switch which reversed the front and rear lights. (J.Fozard)

102. The local cars augmented the frequency of the through cars on the busiest stretches of the tramway, and were useful for local passengers who could often be crowded out by those going 'all the way'. Traffic has to wait until car 23 unloads passengers at the Cayley Arms stop on Rhos seafront. The Penrhyn Avenue terminus of the local trams was shown as 'Church Road' on the destination blind. (J.Fozard)

103. Another view of car 23 on Rhos seafront shows the car at the stop opposite the end of Rhos Road, travelling towards Colwyn Bay. During the later part of their operational careers, both these cars carried paper stickers over the entrance showing the Colwyn Bay local terminal points 'Rhos on Sea' and 'Colwyn Bay'. (J.Fozard)

104. Although Church Road was the terminus of this service, the local cars needed to run forward without passengers for a short distance westwards to the crossover situated outside the depot, Car 24 is about to reverse here, having possibly just left the depot to commence duty on the Colwyn Bay local. The destination blind has probably not been altered since its previous duty. (Roy Brook)

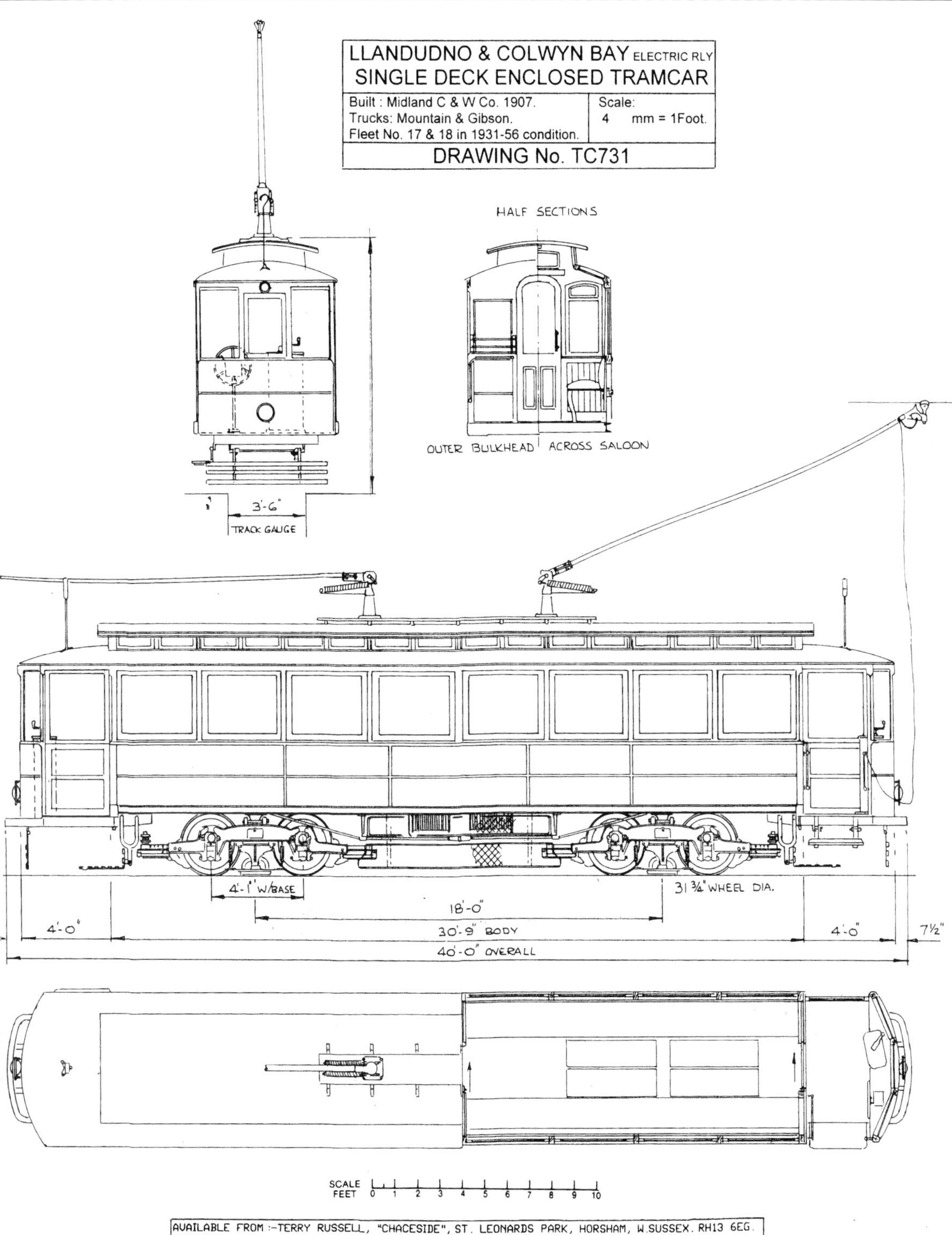
LLANDUDNO & COLWYN BAY ELECTRIC RLY
SINGLE DECK ENCLOSED TRAMCAR
Built : Midland C & W Co. 1907.
Trucks: Mountain & Gibson.
Fleet No. 17 & 18 in 1931-56 condition.
Scale:
4 mm = 1Foot.
DRAWING No. TC731
HALF SECTIONS
OUTER BULKHEAD
ACROSS SALOON
3'-6"
TRACK GAUGE
4'-1" W/BASE
31 3/4" WHEEL DIA.
18'-0"
4'-0"
30'-9" BODY
4'-0"
7½"
40'-0" OVERALL
SCALE
FEET 0 1 2 3 4 5 6 7 8 9 10
AVAILABLE FROM :-TERRY RUSSELL, "CHACESIDE", ST. LEONARDS PARK, HORSHAM, W.SUSSEX. RH13 6EG.
SEND 4 FIRST CLASS STAMPS FOR COMPLETE LIST OF PUBLIC TRANSPORT DRAWINGS.

1 to 14 Original bogie saloon cars

105. The original rolling stock to open the line consisted of fourteen long bogie single deck cars of interurban style. These were built by the Midland Carriage & Wagon Company of Shrewsbury and consisted of an eight-window saloon, split into two compartments, one originally for smokers, with platforms open at each side. Seating was for 42 passengers. The cars were mounted on Mountain and Gibson equal wheel bogies. Some cars were delivered with single trolley poles, but these were very quickly replaced with the double pole arrangement. Originally painted in maroon and cream, these cars assumed an overall grey livery during the Great War, and some never regained the red livery by the time that the green and cream colours were adopted in 1933. In the 1920s, an experiment was carried out using car 14, which was fitted with a bow collector at its Llandudno end, but this was deemed unsuccessful following trials along Penrhyn Avenue. In the early 1930s, a programme of panelling over one side of the open entrances commenced. Cars 1 to 5 were withdrawn when the Accrington cars entered service in 1933, and cars 7, 8, 9, 12 and 13 followed suit at the end of 1936 when the Bournemouth cars arrived. The remaining cars, 6, 10, 11 and 14 were retained and renumbered, their subsequent history being described in the caption to photograph 111. This view shows how the survivors of this type looked in the late 1930s. Note the panelled over platform and the route board which has been moved to a slightly lower position to avoid blocking the view of the newly introduced advertising board. A window bill on the car announces that the Odeon at Colwyn Bay is showing 'Stagecoach' starring John Wayne. This neatly dates the view of renumbered car 16 (formerly car 6) to 1939. (R.Elliott/Tramway and Light Railway Society)

15 to 18 *(top right)*
Single truck 'Yankee' cars

106. This quartet of cars joined the fleet in 1909, and they were very different cars to those of the original fleet. Built by the United Electric Car Company of Preston, they had short fully enclosed bodies with deep windows to American styling – hence their nickname 'Yankees'. Each car was mounted on a Brush Warner radial single truck. They also had destination boxes with roller blind indicators above each platform, and although they entered service with this feature, they were very soon removed as being superfluous to requirements. Being fully enclosed, they were ideal for use in winter (being also known as 'winter cars') and for operation on the two local services at each end of the line. However, the cars were 'semi convertible', and the side windows split in the centre so that the panes could be let into the body, creating a semi-open car for summer use. The radial trucks were replaced by Peckham P35 trucks in 1927, and the whole batch was withdrawn at the end of

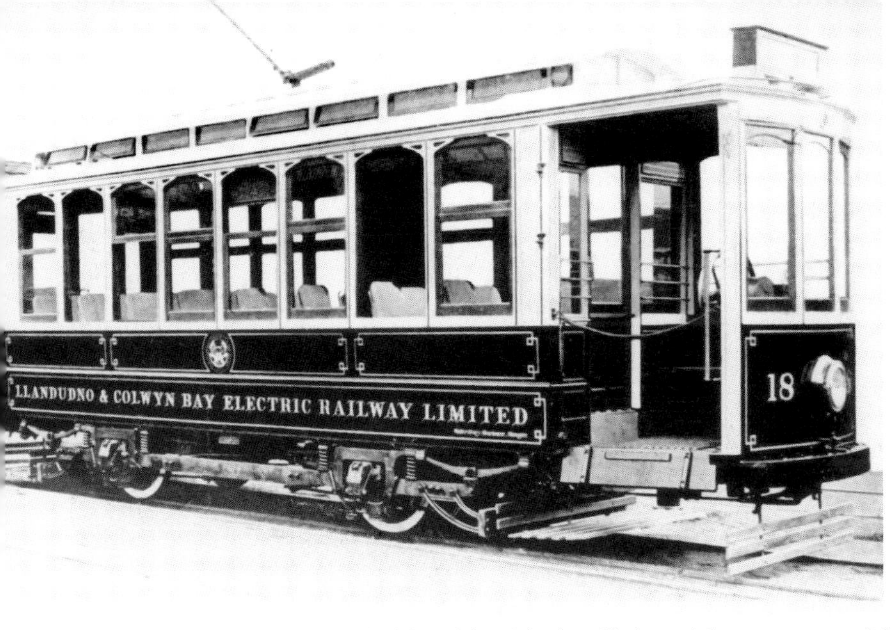

1936. The bodies were stored for some time alongside the depot, and the trucks were sold to Leeds, where they appeared under double deck cars and ran until the 1950s. This official maker's view shows car 18 in the original livery unique to these cars, with two fleet numbers at each end either side of the headlight and the new name of the company shown in full on the rocker panel. These cars did not receive the grey livery mentioned in the previous view, but a single fleet number above the headlight was later applied, and when they received green livery in 1933, the fleet number was smaller than the normal size as shown in photograph 38. (Author's coll.)

19 to 22 Open toastrack cars

107. These very popular cars will be perhaps the ones most remembered by summer visitors to the line. Ordered from the United Electric Car Company (UEC) in 1914, wartime conditions delayed their building, and they were finally delivered in 1920, by which time UEC had been merged into the English Electric company. These cars were of very basic construction, comprising bench seats, mostly reversible, with accommodation for 60 passengers, the highest capacity cars on the line. The equal wheel bogies were built by English Electric to the Mountain and Gibson design. Substantial, but neat V shaped lifeguards were provided at each end. The only significant alteration to these cars was temporary and only affected car 19, which was re-numbered in 1936 to 23 as described in the caption to photograph 113. This official view of car 20 shows it sporting a protruding lifeguard with a net type arrangement. The net was a short lived attachment, although these cars retained the brackets for this fitment on their dashes for some years. All the toastracks were taken out of service at the end of the summer season in September 1955 (see photograph 114). (Author's coll.)

1 to 5 Accrington cars

108. In 1932, five enclosed single deck bogie trams from Accrington Corporation Tramways (4 ft/1219mm gauge) were purchased to replace some of the original cars. These had been built by Brush and had 5 window 40 seat bodies. They were numbered 28 to 32 in the Accrington fleet. The first three dated from 1915, the other two from 1921. Two of the cars (2 and 5) came complete with Brush maximum traction bogie trucks (which required re-gauging), whilst the other three received trucks from the withdrawn cars they replaced. They entered service in 1933 still in Accrington red and cream livery and retained this until about 1936 (see photograph 10). In the early 1950s the wooden seats of these cars were covered with cushions from former Birmingham trams. Cars 1 and 2 were scrapped in early 1956, whilst the remainder survived a short time longer until the closure of the line, cars 3 and 4 operating on the last day. This pre war photograph at the depot shows car 4 (formally Accrington 31) in the green and cream Llandudno livery. (S.G.Jackman/Tramway and Light Railway Society)

6 to 15 Bournemouth open top cars *(lower left)*

109. Further second hand purchases arrived in late 1936 to replace more of the original fleet and the 'Yankee' cars. The first double deck cars to operate on the line, these ten cars became the mainstay of operations until the end. Originating from Bournemouth Corporation Tramways (3ft 6 ins/1067mm gauge), all ten cars looked alike, but were in fact from various batches of cars built between 1914 and 1928. The individual building dates, with Bournemouth fleet number in brackets, were:

6 (85) 1914	11 (95) 1921
7 (115) 1925	12 (128) 1928
8 (116) 1925	13 (112) 1921
9 (108) 1921	14 (121) 1925
10 (103) 1921	15 (114) 1925

Apart from car 6, which was built by the United Electric Car Company, all the cars were built by Brush and all had Brill 22E maximum traction bogies. The motors and controllers varied considerably in type and manufacturer. The four window bodies seated 56. All entered service in Llandudno green and cream livery, and it is thought that the cars were painted thus before leaving Bournemouth. No substantial outward alteration was made to these cars whilst in Llandudno. Cars 9 and 10 were scrapped in January 1956, but all the others ran until the end, with car 8 being the last car of all. Car 6 was saved for preservation (see photograph 118). This view shows car 11 at West Shore on Whit Sunday 1951. At this time the car carried two crests on each side of the car. The only other car to do this was car 12. (J.F.Henton)

23, 24 Darwen streamline cars

110. The final additions to the company's rolling stock were this pair of double deck air-braked cars bought from Darwen Corporation in 1946. These 60 seaters were built by English Electric to the streamlined design also supplied to Blackpool and Sunderland, although their appearance differed to these due to the narrow body construction, (Darwen's tracks were 4 foot gauge). This resulted in the cars having rather upright front ends. When new, they were known as 'Queen Marys' after the Cunard liner which also entered service in 1936. Becoming surplus to requirements at Darwen shortly before the system closed, the L&CBER snapped them up and they were delivered to the depot in August 1946. The English Electric maximum traction bogies were sent away for re-gauging, and the cars were not ready for service until April 1948. Although numbered 23 and 24 in Darwen, their Llandudno numbers were 24 and 23 respectively. These cars were not a success and after two seasons or so had to be withdrawn from Llandudno due to their rough riding on the poor track, which also damaged the air brake fittings. From the early 1950s they were restricted to operation between Church Road and Colwyn Bay terminus and by the end of 1953 they had been withdrawn, languishing in the depot until the end of tram operation. Unrealised hopes of a sale to Blackpool resulted in these fascinating cars being the last of all to be broken up, in early 1957. Car 24 (ex Darwen 23) is seen at the depot with the nearside staircase visible inside the central entrance. (Author's coll.)

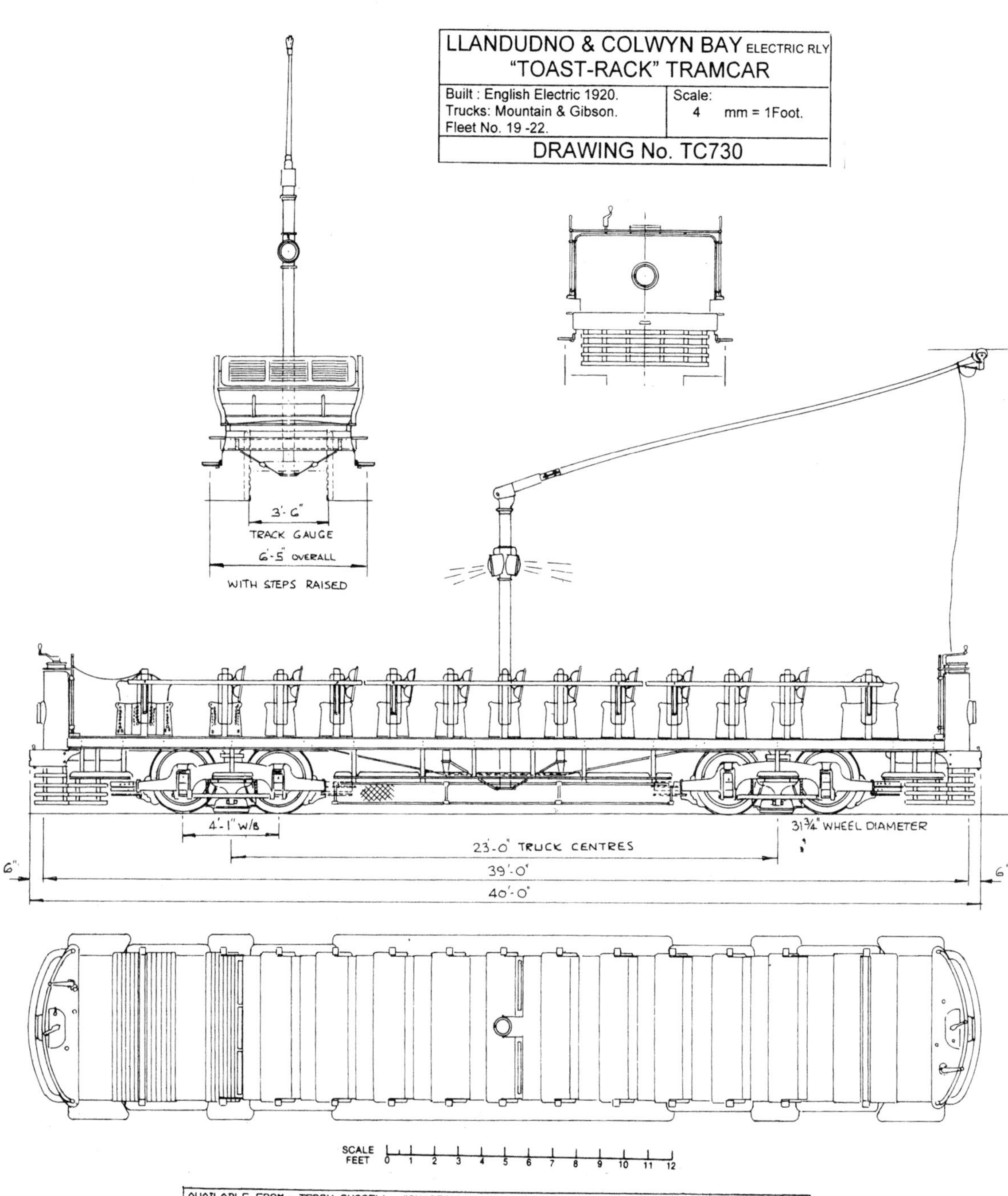

AVAILABLE FROM :-TERRY RUSSELL, "CHACESIDE", ST. LEONARDS PARK, HORSHAM, W.SUSSEX. RH13 6EG.
SEND 4 FIRST CLASS STAMPS FOR COMPLETE LIST OF PUBLIC TRANSPORT DRAWINGS.

RENUMBERING

111. As described in the caption to photograph 105, four of the original bogie saloon cars were retained following the influx of the Bournemouth cars in late 1936. The cars involved were originally numbered 6, 10, 11 and 14 and these were renumbered 16, 19, 17 and 18 respectively. The actual date of renumbering is unclear. This photograph, dated 9th June 1938, shows, from the left, renumbered car 17 (formerly 11), works car 23, which was itself renumbered 23A, when the Darwen cars arrived in 1946, and original car 14, which is still awaiting renumbering to become 18. The subsequent fortunes of these cars varied greatly. Car 19 (10) was withdrawn to be converted into a toastrack type car, but this was never completed and the car was scrapped in the late 1930s. It is doubtful whether it ever ran as 19. Car 16 (6) ran until 1945, when an overheating axlebox caused it to be gutted by fire at Bodafon Fields and it never ran again. Car 17 (11) ran until the final year of operation, whilst car 18 (14) lasted until the very end, although it was not available for service in the final days. (D.W.K.Jones/National Tramway Museum)

Construction car 23

In 1930 a works car was bought from the Leamington and Warwick tramways. Before this, the company did not possess a tram of this type. It was a former 1901 built single-truck passenger car which had originated with the Taunton tramways and was used at Llandudno until 1936, when it was removed from its truck and dumped beside the depot. It was replaced with another 1901 built car from Bournemouth, which had originated with the Poole and District electric tramways. This had a GF Milnes body with Brill 21E truck. Converted by Bournemouth into works car with rail grinding equipment, it had a bizarre appearance due to the removal of the top deck but retention of the staircases! Painted overall grey, numbered 23 and lettered 'L&CBER Construction Car' in white on each dash, the car survived until the end of the system. On the arrival of ex Darwen car 23 in 1946, the construction car was numbered 23A.

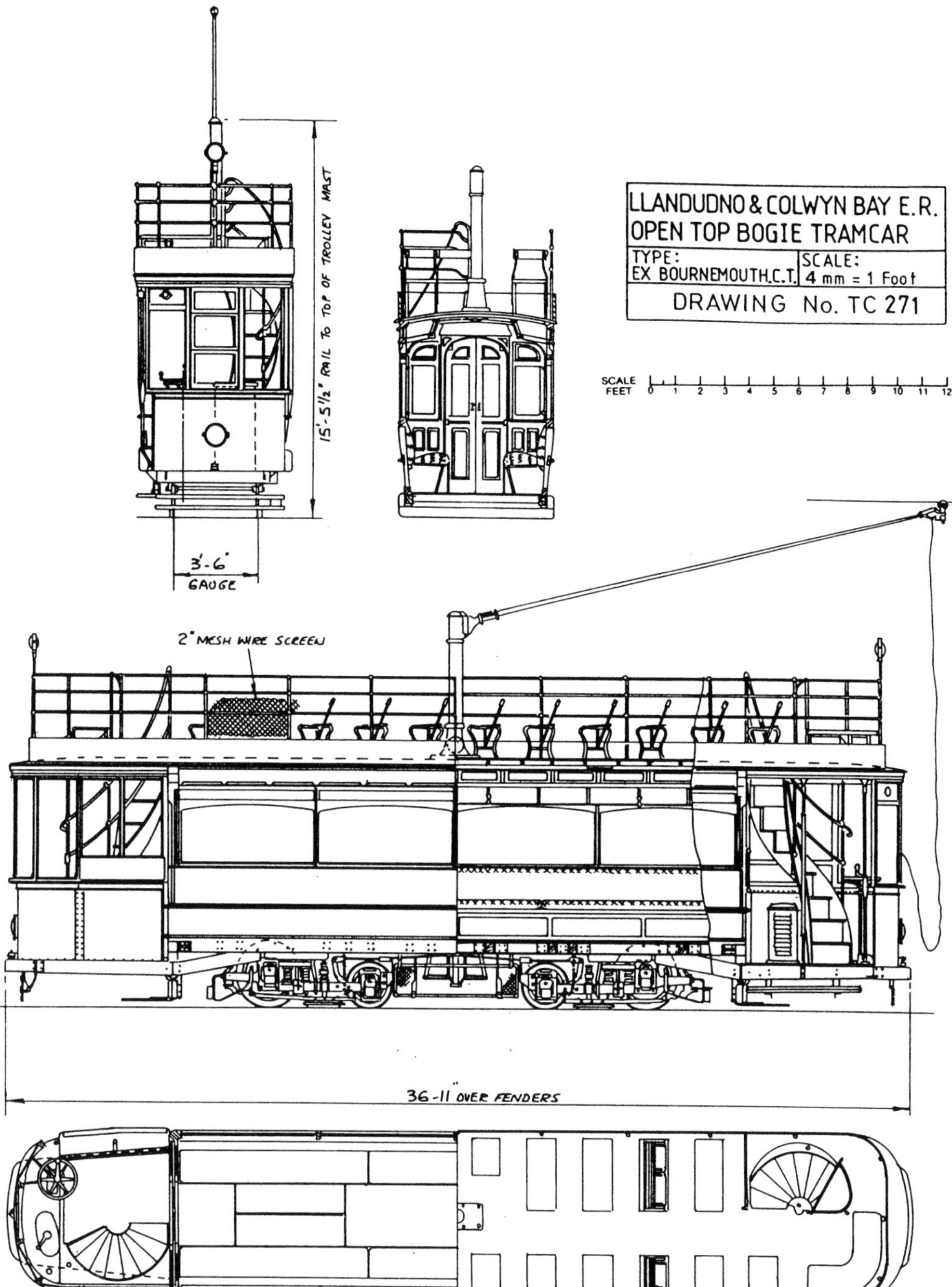

BUILT BY BRUSH IN 1921 TO 1926 FOR BOURNEMOUTH CORP. TWYS PURCHASED BY L+CBER IN 1936. FLEET Nos AS FOLLOWS B.C.T Nos IN BRACKETS : 13 (112), 7 (115), 8 (116), 9 (108), 10 (103), 11 (95), 12 (128), 14 (121), 15 (114).

No. 6 (85) IS SIMILAR BUT HAS SEMI-CIRCULAR UPPER DECK ENDS AND IS PRESERVED IN B.C.T CONDITION.

112. The renumbering of car 10 to 19, as described in the previous photograph, resulted in the existing toastrack car 19 in turn being renumbered to 23. This rare view shows the car as 23 at West Shore in the late 1930s. The conductor is raising the guard rails and the running board steps. The driver is probably reversing the process on the other side, before placing the controller handle on the front of the car. This was part of the familiar procedure at each terminus with this type of car. (E.G.Cope/L&CBTS coll./Conwy Archive Service)

113. Toastrack car 23 soon reverted to its former number 19 when the renumbered bogie saloon car 19 was withdrawn. As a contrast to the previous photograph, the car is seen here at West Shore in 1947, with the passengers settling down in their seats, whilst the conductor attends to his duties. Conductors had to volunteer to work this type of car, and were not supposed to collect fares whilst the car was on the move. (A.E.Old)

FINALE

114. 1955 was to be the last full year of tram operation, the summer season ending at the end of September. This meant that the toastrack cars would disappear from service for good. By this time, these were the last of this traditional design of tourist tram left in operation on British roads. On 25th September, a special enthusiasts' tour was arranged, and this would be the final occasion that these cars ran. Car 21 is seen during this event at Church Road, Penrhyn Avenue, being passed by Accrington car 2. (R.J.S.Wiseman)

115. The final day of operation was Saturday, 24th March 1956. Bournemouth car 8 was the designated last car, which carried the official party and, driven by Chief Inspector Woolley, arrived back at the depot in the early hours of Sunday. Earlier on the last day, this car had been used by a party of former Bournemouth tram drivers, enabling them to have a last drive of one of 'their' cars. Later on Sunday, it is seen here posed in the depot yard, still carrying the chalked 'Last car' message on the dash panel. Alongside is Red Bus no 3, one of the replacement ex Southdown Guy Arab buses, painted in a dark red and cream livery. Note that it is carrying the company crest on its side. This was a short lived adornment, and was not perpetuated once the initial supply of transfers was used up. Latterly the only clue to ownership was the small legal lettering beside the nearside front wheel. (J.Copland /C.W.Routh)

L&CBER TRAM PARTS USED ON SEATON TRAMWAYS CARS

Car 2 (Built 1963/4 Metropolitan Tramways style open top). Parts of L&CBER ex Bournemouth cars used in the construction of bulkheads and sliding doors; self aligning trolleyhead ex Birmingham sold to L&CBER 1952/3 and latterly carried by cars 1-5.

Car 4 (Built 1961 Blackpool style open boat car). Motorman's air brake valves, air whistles, controllers and circuit breakers from the ex Darwen cars.

Car 6 (1954, rebuilt 1956, 1962, 1989 Bournemouth/L&CBER style open top). Top deck seats and scroll work ex Bournemouth car 8 (L&CBER's last tram), headlamps, gongs, signal bells and circuit breakers from various other L&CBER cars. This car was displayed on the former track bed of the L&CBER at Bodafon Fields in May 1996.

Car 7 (1958 Bournemouth/L&CBER style open top) Top deck seats from ex Bournemouth cars, headlamps, gongs, signal bells, circuit breakers from various L&CBER cars and the controllers from L&CBER no 3 (ex Accrington).

Car 12 (1966, rebuilt 1980 and 1999. Feltham style open top) The other pair of controllers from the ex Darwen cars.

RED BUSES

116. Having decided to replace the trams with buses, the company purchased this former East Kent Leyland Titan 1938 built double decker in September 1955 for driver training. It was painted in the dark red and cream livery and is seen here in Mostyn Street, Llandudno, under the tram wires, on October 1st 1955. At this time it was expected that the trams would be withdrawn by the end of the year. This bus never ran in passenger service and was disposed of soon after the tramway conversion. (J.Copland /C.W.Routh)

117. The original Red Bus fleet comprised thirteen vehicles, all but two being ex Southdown utility Guy Arabs, with various makes of bodywork. The other two, numbered 1 and 2 in the fleet, were open top Daimler COG5 vehicles with Northern Coachbuilders bodywork originating from Newcastle Corporation. Contrary to what might be expected, these had been converted to open top configuration at Newcastle some years before their sojourn to North Wales, and they had operated as such in Newcastle. No 1 is seen in this busy scene at West Shore terminus in 1960, with an ex Southdown Guy behind it. Alongside is a competing cream liveried Crosville Bristol Lodekka open top bus operating on the through service to Old Colwyn and Penmaen Head. At its farther end beyond Colwyn Bay, this route was the replacement for the Old Colwyn tram service. The bus itself is almost new, Crosville tending to run their latest vehicles to compete with the tram company's elderly vehicles. Remarkably, this particular bus, 627 HFM, still exists and is fully restored to full PCV operating condition in Cumbria. (R.Marshall)

POSTSCRIPT

118. The only company tram to escape scrapping was Bournemouth car 6, which was purchased privately and presented to the Museum of British Transport in London where it was displayed in the early 1960s. The car is now fully restored to its original identity as Bournemouth 85, and is resident at the Electricity Museum in Christchurch, Dorset, near the terminus of the former tram route from Bournemouth. This view shows the car on display at the Museum of British Transport, which was housed in a former tram depot at Clapham. The car is in the condition in which it last ran at Llandudno. (D.F.Parker)

119. Relics of the tramway survive in individual collections. This typical shield shaped sign was once affixed to a traction pole at West Shore terminus. Note that the inappropriate use of the apostrophe is not a present day phenomenon! (D.Jones)

120. A tram returned to the streets of Llandudno and Colwyn Bay in 2007 to celebrate the centenary of the line. The Llandudno & Colwyn Bay Tramway Society (L&CBTS) has created this replica of ex Bournemouth car 7 using the lower deck remains of Bournemouth tram 126 (a car that was not sold to the L&CBER, although being of the same type). The replica car 7 will be exhibited extensively in the area throughout centenary year. The society's longer term aim is to create a fully operational L&CBER car using the body from Bournemouth car 86. 'New' car 7 is seen here on on 7th May 2007 being displayed at the Victorian Extravaganza in Llandudno, shortly before the fitment of the headlamps on the front dashes. The L&CBTS is committed to keeping the memory of the tramway alive and full details of their activities are contained on their website:

www.swissitalianpaddlesteamers.com/lcbtramsoc/home

(Geoff Price Lancaster)

EVOLVING THE ULTIMATE RAIL ENCYCLOPEDIA

Easebourne Lane, Midhurst, West Sussex.
GU29 9AZ Tel:01730 813169
www.middletonpress.co.uk email:info@middletonpress.co.uk
A-978 0 906520 B- 978 1 873793 C- 978 1 901706 D-978 1 904474 E - 978 1 906008

OOP Out of print at time of printing - Please check availability BROCHURE AVAILABLE SHOWING NEW TITLES

A
Abergavenny to Merthyr C 91 8
Abertillery and Ebbw Vale Lines D 84 5
Aldgate & Stepney Tramways B 70 1
Allhallows - Branch Line to A 62 8
Alton - Branch Lines to A 11 6
Andover to Southampton A 82 6
Ascot - Branch Lines around A 64 2
Ashburton - Branch Line to B 95 4
Ashford - Steam to Eurostar B 67 1
Ashford to Dover A 48 2
Austrian Narrow Gauge D 04 3
Avonmouth - BL around D 42 5
Aylesbury to Rugby D 91 3
B
Baker Street to Uxbridge D 90 6
Banbury to Birmingham D 27 2
Barking to Southend C 80 2
Barnet & Finchley Tramways B 93 0
Barry - Branch Lines around D 50 0
Basingstoke to Salisbury A 89 5
Bath Green Park to Bristol C 36 9
Bath to Evercreech Junction A 60 4
Bath Tramways B 86 2
Battle over Portsmouth 1940 A 29 1
Battle over Sussex 1940 A 79 6
Bedford to Wellingborough D 31 9
Betwixt Petersfield & Midhurst A 94 9
Bletchley to Cambridge D 94 4
Bletchley to Rugby E 07 9
Blitz over Sussex 1941-42 B 35 0
Bodmin - Branch Lines around B 83 1
Bognor at War 1939-45 B 59 6
Bombers over Sussex 1943-45 B 51 0
Bournemouth & Poole Trys B 47 3
Bournemouth to Evercreech Jn A 46 8
Bournemouth to Weymouth A 57 4 OOP
Bournemouth Trolleybuses C 10 9
Bradford Trolleybuses D 19 7
Brecon to Neath D 43 2
Brecon to Newport D 16 6
Brecon to Newtown E 06 2
Brickmaking in Sussex B 19 6 OOP
Brightons Tramways B 02 2 OOP
Brighton to Eastbourne A 16 1
Brighton to Worthing A 03 1
Brighton Trolleybuses D 34 0
Bristols Tramways B 57 2
Bristol to Taunton D 03 6
Bromley South to Rochester B 23 7
Bromsgrove to Birmingham D 87 6
Bromsgrove to Gloucester D 73 9
Brunel - A railtour of his achievements D 74 6
Bude - Branch Line to B 29 9
Burnham to Evercreech Jn A 68 0
Burton & Ashby Tramways C 51 2
C
Camberwell & West Norwood Tys B 22 0
Cambridge to Ely D 55 5
Canterbury - Branch Lines around B 58 9
Cardiff Trolleybuses D 64 7
Caterham & Tattenham Corner B 25 1
Changing Midhurst C 15 4
Chard and Yeovil - BLs around C 30 7
Charing Cross to Dartford A 75 8
Charing Cross to Orpington A 96 3
Cheddar - Branch Line to B 90 9
Cheltenham to Andover C 43 7
Cheltenham to Redditch D 81 4
Chesterfield Tramways D 37 1
Chesterfield Trolleybuses D 51 7
Chester Tramways E 04 8
Chichester to Portsmouth A 14 7
Clapham & Streatham Trys B 97 8
Clapham Junction - 50 yrs C 06 2 OOP
Clapham Junction to Beckenham Jn B 36 7
Cleobury Mortimer - Branch Lines around E 18 5
Clevedon & Portishead - BLs to D 18 0
Collectors Trains, Trolleys & Trams D 29 6
Colonel Stephens D62 3
Cornwall Narrow Gauge D 56 2
Cowdray & Easebourne D 96 8
Crawley to Littlehampton A 34 5
Cromer - Branch Lines around C 26 6
Croydons Tramways B 42 8
Croydons Trolleybuses B 73 2 OOP
Croydon to East Grinstead B 48 0
Crystal Palace (HL) & Catford Loop A 87 1
Cyprus Narrow Gauge E13 0
D
Darlington to Newcastle D 98 2
Darlington Trolleybuses D 33 3
Dartford to Sittingbourne B 34 3
Derby Tramways D 17 3
Derby Trolleybuses C 72 7
Derwent Valley - Branch Line to the D 06 7
Devon Narrow Gauge E 09 3
Didcot to Banbury D 02 9
Didcot to Swindon C 84 0
Didcot to Winchester C 13 0
Dorset & Somerset Narrow Gauge D 76 0
Douglas to Peel C 88 8
Douglas to Port Erin C 55 0
Douglas to Ramsey D 39 5
Dovers Tramways B 24 4
Dover to Ramsgate A 78 9
E
Ealing to Slough C 42 0
Eastbourne to Hastings A 27 7 OOP
East Cornwall Mineral Railways D 22 7
East Croydon to Three Bridges A 53 6
East Grinstead - Branch Lines to A 07 9
East Ham & West Ham Tramways B 52 7
East Kent Light Railway A 61 1 OOP
East London - Branch Lines of C 44 4
East London Line B 80 0
East Ridings Secret Resistance D 21 0
Edgware & Willesden Tramways C 18 5
Effingham Junction - BLs around A 74 1
Eltham & Woolwich Tramways B 74 9 OOP
Ely to Kings Lynn C 53 6
Ely to Norwich C 90 1
Embankment & Waterloo Tramways B 41 1
Enfield & Wood Green Trys C 03 1 OOP
Enfield Town & Palace Gates - BL to D 32 6
Epsom to Horsham A 30 7
Euston to Harrow & Wealdstone C 89 5
Exeter & Taunton Tramways B 32 9
Exeter to Barnstaple B 15 2
Exeter to Newton Abbot C 49 9
Exeter to Tavistock B 69 5
Exmouth - Branch Lines to B 00 8
F
Fairford - Branch Line to A 52 9
Falmouth, Helston & St. Ives - BL to C 74 1
Fareham to Salisbury A 67 3
Faversham to Dover B 05 3
Felixstowe & Aldeburgh - BL to D 20 3
Fenchurch Street to Barking C 20 8
Festiniog - 50 yrs of enterprise C 83 3
Festiniog 1946-55 E 01 7 - PUB 21 APRIL
Festiniog in the Fifties B 68 8
Festiniog in the Sixties B 91 6
Finsbury Park to Alexandra Palace C 02 4
Frome to Bristol B 77 0
Fulwell - Trams, Trolleys & Buses D 11 1
G
Gloucester to Bristol D 35 7
Gloucester to Cardiff D 66 1
Gosport & Horndean Trys B 92 3
Gosport - Branch Lines around A 36 9
Great Yarmouth Tramways D 13 5
Greece Narrow Gauge D 72 2
Greenwich & Dartford Tramways B 14 5 OOP
Grimsby & Cleethorpes Trolleybuses D 86 9
Guildford to Redhill A 63 5 OOP
H
Hammersmith & Hounslow Trys C 33 8
Hampshire Narrow Gauge D 36 4
Hampshire Waterways A 84 0 OOP
Hampstead & Highgate Tramways B 53 4
Harrow to Watford D 14 2
Hastings to Ashford A 37 6
Hastings Tramways B 18 3
Hastings Trolleybuses B 81 7 OOP
Hawkhurst - Branch Line to A 66 6
Hay-on-Wye - Branch Lines around D 92 0
Hayling - Branch Line to A 12 3
Haywards Heath to Seaford A 28 4
Hemel Hempstead - Branch Lines to D 88 3
Henley, Windsor & Marlow - BL to C77 2
Hereford to Newport D 54 8
Hexham to Carlisle D 75 3
Hitchin to Peterborough D 07 4
Holborn & Finsbury Tramways B 79 4
Holborn Viaduct to Lewisham A 81 9
Horsham - Branch Lines to A 02 4
Huddersfield Tramways D 95 1
Huddersfield Trolleybuses C 92 5
Hull Tramways D60 9
Hull Trolleybuses D 24 1
Huntingdon - Branch Lines around A 93 2
I
Ilford & Barking Tramways B 61 9
Ilford to Shenfield C 97 0
Ilfracombe - Branch Line to B 21 3
Ilkeston & Glossop Tramways D 40 1
Industrial Rlys of the South East A 09 3
Ipswich to Saxmundham C 41 3
Ipswich Trolleybuses D 59 3
Isle of Wight Lines - 50 yrs C 12 3
K
Keighley Tramways & Trolleybuses D 83 8
Kent & East Sussex Waterways A 72 X
Kent Narrow Gauge C 45 1
Kent Seaways - Hoys to Hovercraft D 79 1
Kidderminster to Shrewsbury E10 9
Kingsbridge - Branch Line to C 98 7
Kingston & Hounslow Loops A 83 3 OOP
Kingston & Wimbledon Tramways B 56 5
Kingswear - Branch Line to C 17 8
L
Lambourn - Branch Line to C 70 3
Launceston & Princetown - BL to C 19 2
Lewisham & Catford Tramways B 26 8 OOP
Lewisham to Dartford A 92 5
Lines around Wimbledon B 75 6
Liverpool Street to Chingford D 01 2
Liverpool Street to Ilford C 34 5
Liverpool Tramways - Eastern C 04 8
Liverpool Tramways - Northern C 46 8
Liverpool Tramways - Southern C 23 9
Llandudno & Colwyn Bay Tramways E 17 8
London Bridge to Addiscombe B 20 6
London Bridge to East Croydon A 58 1
London Chatham & Dover Railway A 88 8
London Termini - Past and Proposed D 00 5
London to Portsmouth Waterways B 43 5
Longmoor - Branch Lines to A 41 3
Looe - Branch Line to C 22 2
Ludlow to Hereford E 14 7
Lyme Regis - Branch Line to A 45 1
Lynton - Branch Line to B 04 6
M
Maidstone & Chatham Tramways B 40 4
Maidstone Trolleybuses C 00 0 OOP
March - Branch Lines around B 09 1
Margate & Ramsgate Tramways C 52 9
Marylebone to Rickmansworth D49 4
Melton Constable to Yarmouth Beach E 03 1
Midhurst - Branch Lines around A 49 9
Midhurst - Branch Lines to A 01 7 OOP
Military Defence of West Sussex A 23 9
Military Signals, South Coast C 54 3
Minehead - Branch Line to A 80 2
Mitcham Junction Lines B 01 5
Mitchell & company C 59 8
Monmouthshire Eastern Valleys D 71 5
Moreton-in-Marsh to Worcester D 26 5
Moretonhampstead - BL to C 27 7
Mountain Ash to Neath D 80 7
N
Newbury to Westbury C 66 6
Newcastle to Hexham D 69 2
Newcastle Trolleybuses D 78 4
Newport (IOW) - Branch Lines to A 26 0
Newquay - Branch Lines to C 71 0
Newton Abbot to Plymouth C 60 4
Northern France Narrow Gauge C 75 8
North East German Narrow Gauge D 44 9
North Kent Tramways B 44 2
North London Line B 94 7
North Woolwich - BLs around C 65 9
Norwich Tramways C 40 6
Nottinghamshire & Derbyshire T/B D 63 0
Nottinghamshire & Derbyshire T/W D 53 1
O
Ongar - Branch Lines to E 05 5
Orpington to Tonbridge B 03 9 OOP
Oxford to Bletchley D57 9
Oxford to Moreton-in-Marsh D 15 9
P
Paddington to Ealing C 37 6
Paddington to Princes Risborough C 81 9
Padstow - Branch Line to B 54 1
Plymouth - BLs around B 98 5
Plymouth to St. Austell C 63 5
Pontypool to Mountain Ash D 65 4
Porthmadog 1954-94 - BL around B 31 2
Porthmadog to Blaenau B 50 3 OOP
Portmadoc 1923-46 - BL around B 13 8
Portsmouths Tramways B 72 5
Portsmouth to Southampton A 31 4
Portsmouth Trolleybuses C 73 4
Potters Bar to Cambridge D 70 8
Princes Risborough - Branch Lines to D 05 0
Princes Risborough to Banbury C 85 7
R
Railways to Victory C 16 1 OOP
Reading to Basingstoke B 27 5
Reading to Didcot C 79 6
Reading to Guildford A 47 5 OOP
Reading Tramways B 87 9
Reading Trolleybuses C 05 5
Redhill to Ashford A 73 4
Return to Blaenau 1970-82 C 64 2
Rickmansworth to Aylesbury D 61 6
Roman Roads of Hampshire D 67 8
Roman Roads of Kent E 02 4
Roman Roads of Surrey C 61 1
Roman Roads of Sussex C 48 2
Romneyrail C 32 1
Ryde to Ventnor A 19 2
S
Salisbury to Westbury B 39 8
Salisbury to Yeovil B 06 0 OOP
Saxmundham to Yarmouth C 69 7
Saxony Narrow Gauge D 47 0
Scarborough Tramways E 15 4
Seaton & Eastbourne Tramways B 76 3 OOP
Seaton & Sidmouth - Branch Lines to A 95 6
Secret Sussex Resistance B 82 4
SECR Centenary album C 11 6 OOP
Selsey - Branch Line to A 04 8
Sheerness - Branch Lines around B 16 9 OOP
Shepherds Bush to Uxbridge T/Ws C 28 4
Shrewsbury - Branch Line to A 86 4
Sierra Leone Narrow Gauge D 28 9
Sirhowy Valley Line E 12 3
Sittingbourne to Ramsgate A 90 1
Slough to Newbury C 56 7
Solent - Creeks, Crafts & Cargoes D 52 4
Southamptons Tramways B 33 6
Southampton to Bournemouth A 42 0
Southend-on-Sea Tramways B 28 2
Southern France Narrow Gauge C 47 5
Southwark & Deptford Tramways B 38 1
Southwold - Branch Line to A 15 4
South Eastern & Chatham Railways C 08 6
South London Line B 46 6
South London Tramways 1903-33 D 10 4
South London Tramways 1933-52 D 89 0
South Shields Trolleybuses E 11 6
St. Albans to Bedford D 08 1
St. Austell to Penzance C 67 3
St. Pancras to Barking D 68 5
St. Pancras to St. Albans C 78 9
Stamford Hill Tramways B 85 5
Steaming through Cornwall B 30 5 OOP
Steaming through Kent A 13 0 OOP
Steaming through the Isle of Wight A 56 7
Steaming through West Hants A 69 7
Stratford upon avon to Birmingham D 77 7
Stratford upon Avon to Cheltenham C 25 3
Strood to Paddock Wood B 12 1 OOP
Surrey Home Guard C 57 4
Surrey Narrow Gauge C 87 1
Surrey Waterways A 51 2 OOP
Sussex Home Guard C 24 6
Sussex Narrow Gauge C 68 0
Sussex Shipping Sail, Steam & Motor D 23 4 C
Swanley to Ashford B 45 9
Swindon to Bristol C 96 3
Swindon to Gloucester D46 3
Swindon to Newport D 30 2
Swiss Narrow Gauge C 94 9
T
Talyllyn - 50 years C 39 0
Taunton to Barnstaple B 60 2
Taunton to Exeter C 82 6
Tavistock to Plymouth B 88 6
Tees-side Trolleybuses D 58 6
Tenterden - Branch Line to A 21 5
Thanets Tramways B 11 4 OOP
Three Bridges to Brighton A 35 2
Tilbury Loop C 86 4
Tiverton - Branch Lines around C 62 8
Tivetshall to Beccles D 41 8
Tonbridge to Hastings A 44 4
Torrington - Branch Lines to B 37 4
Tunbridge Wells - Branch Lines to A 32 1
Twickenham & Kingston Trys C 35 2
Two-Foot Gauge Survivors C 21 5 OOP
U
Upwell - Branch Line to B 64 0
V
Victoria & Lambeth Tramways B 49 7
Victoria to Bromley South A 98 7
Victoria to East Croydon A 40 6 OOP
Vivarais C 31 4 OOP
Vivarais Revisited E 08 6
W
Walthamstow & Leyton Tramways B 65 7
Waltham Cross & Edmonton Trys C 07 9
Wandsworth & Battersea Tramways B 63 3
Wantage - Branch Line to D 25 8
Wareham to Swanage - 50 yrs D 09 8
War on the Line A 10 9
War on the Line VIDEO + 88 0
Waterloo to Windsor A 54 3
Waterloo to Woking A 38 3
Watford to Leighton Buzzard D 45 6
Wenford Bridge to Fowey C 09 3
Westbury to Bath B 55 8
Westbury to Taunton C 76 5
West Cornwall Mineral Railways D 48 7
West Croydon to Epsom B 08 4
West German Narrow Gauge D 93 7
West London - Branch Lines of C 50 5
West London Line B 84 8
West Sussex Waterways A 24 6 OOP
West Wiltshire - Branch Lines of D 12 8
Weymouth - Branch Lines around A 65 9
Willesden Junction to Richmond B 71 8
Wimbledon to Beckenham C 58 1
Wimbledon to Epsom B 62 6
Wimborne - Branch Lines around A 97 0
Wisbech - Branch Lines around C 01 7
Wisbech 1800-1901 C 93 2
Woking to Alton A 59 8
Woking to Portsmouth A 25 3
Woking to Southampton A 55 0
Wolverhampton Trolleybuses D 85 2
Woolwich & Dartford Trolleys B 66 4
Worcester to Birmingham D 97 5
Worcester to Hereford D 38 8
Worthing to Chichester A 06 2
Y
Yeovil - 50 yrs change C 38 3
Yeovil to Dorchester A 76 5 OOP
Yeovil to Exeter A 91 8
York Tramways & Trolleybuses D 82 1